PRAISE FOR
YEAH, BUT WHAT
ABOUT *THIS* KID?

"Yeah, But What About *This* Kid?, *is not for the faint of heart—but for those educators who have the* **biggest hearts**, *and real determination to look strategically at their instructional practices, classroom management, student engagement, and individual students' needs. It's for those who ask themselves, "Is what I am doing really working for my kids?" The many clearly defined scenarios in this book will lead to in-depth, diagnostic conversations on what is best for our students. Today's instructional leaders of all levels need to read this book."*

> Libby Sluder
> *ESEA Improvement Specialist*
> Mesa Public Schools, Mesa, AZ

"*Authors Grace Dearborn and Scott Sturgeon manage to share their personal chronicles of how schools and districts are activating, at scale, the engagement and achievement of our most impenetrable cohort of learners. This book is an essential read for all professional educators of conscience who've found themselves wondering:* Yeah, But What About *This* Kid?"

> Paul Kilkenny
> *Mentor Teacher*
> *Science Curriculum Coordinator*
> East Side Union High School District, San Jose, CA

"Finally, a book that clearly and concisely explains how to work with your most difficult students. Grace and Scott say that changing poor behavior is like changing a bad habit—it's hard! Luckily, Yeah, But What About *This* Kid? *makes it possible. This book is a "must have" for any teacher who cares enough for his or her students to see that challenging behavior is really a request for love, attention, and validation—and is willing to learn step-by-step techniques to help give those students the support they need."*

Ramona Priester
On-Site Instructional Coach
Victor Elementary School District, Victorville, CA

"It's here! This is the book we have all been waiting for. It provides educators in the trenches with practical solutions to real issues in the classroom."

Kelly C. Chavez
On-Site Instructional Coordinator
Victor Elementary School District, Victorville, CA

"This book is the answer to all of those times you have thought, "I have tried everything, and nothing works with this student." Grace and Scott look at the reasons behind challenging behaviors and give practical strategies for overcoming them. This book should be in every teacher's professional library!"

Michelle Bishop
Instructional Coach
Boise Independent School District, Boise, ID

"With 27 years of experience and much of that focused on 'those kids,' I felt I had as much success as anyone in keeping my classroom engaging and productive. However, after reading and implementing the practices in Yeah, But What About *This* Kid?*, it's moved up to a whole new level. One of the best things I've done for myself and my students was to read this book."*

Dwayne Tubbs
Restorative Justice Director / Teacher
Hanford Joint Union High School District, Hanford, CA

"This book is an excellent resource for a school community to utilize as they attempt to develop a building culture to support each and every student. It provides not only the why, but more importantly the how, of intervening with the most challenging students on a school campus."

Myra Brown
Special Ed Induction Specialist
Mesa County Valley School District 51, Grand Junction, CO

*"*Yeah, But What About *This* Kid? *gives practical perspective and tips for anyone who serves students. It empowers educators to take a look at student behaviors as needs, not problems. It should be in every school office and in every staff room.*

Liz Ybarra
Coordinator of Elementary Programs
Brentwood Union School District, Brentwood, CA

Yeah, But What About *This* Kid?
Tier 3 Behavior Interventions That Work
By Grace Dearborn & Scott Sturgeon

Published by Conscious Teaching, LLC
21 Crest Road
Fairfax, CA 94930
Phone: 415.456.9190
Email: support@consciousteaching.com
Website: www.consciousteaching.com

I.S.B.N. 978-0-9796355-7-1
Library of Congress card number pending.

Cover Design: Alexis Clark
Cartoons: Ruxandra Șerbănoiu
Book Design: Alexis Clark
Copy Editing: Kristin Donnan, Rockin' Dog Studio
Printed in the United States of America

Yeah, But What About *This* Kid?

Tier 3 Behavior Interventions That Work

GRACE DEARBORN

SCOTT STURGEON

TABLE OF CONTENTS

FOREWORD

If you are a teacher or an administrator who has ever struggled to reach that one student — the student with whom nothing seems to work — this is the book for you.

Whether you work in an urban center, the suburbs, or in a rural district, you will often have students who have challenges that you might not be prepared to deal with. This is true even if your college or university offered training in the areas of classroom management and behavior intervention, or if your school district has contributed some of its limited resources to professional development on these topics. In the end, despite everyone's best efforts, we still struggle with our students who have the hardest time focusing, following directions, and responding appropriately to us — our Tier 3 students. These are our neediest students, but they are also the students we may be least prepared to help and whom we are most likely to fail.

Until now.

In *Yeah, But What About* This *Kid?* Grace and Scott offer some of the missing attitudes, tools, and techniques that teachers and administrators need to support their most vulnerable students. They start by peeling away mindsets and assumptions that are counterproductive when working with challenging students, and building up positive replacement beliefs that can turn students from confrontational to cooperative. They also offer practical strategies and realistic interventions that classroom teachers, school site administrators, and on-site specialists can implement immediately to address the needs of their most explosive, hostile, and/or disengaged students.

This book offers a road map for how to shift a school's climate and culture, revamp discipline systems, de-escalate volatile situations, and create short- and long-term interventions that work. Grace and Scott keep it real. You will find real-life scenarios, straight talk, concrete solutions, and hope.

Dr. Todd Whitaker
Professor of Education
University of Missouri

Author of:

Your First Year: How to Survive and Thrive as a New Teacher

School Culture Rewired: How to Define, Assess, and Transform It

Shifting the Monkey

What Great Teachers Do Differently: 17 Things that Matter Most

What Great Principals Do Differently: 18 Things that Matter Most

And more...

ACKNOWLEDGEMENTS

We are honored to have received invaluable help from many people in bringing this labor of love to print. To our dozens of preview readers from across the country, thank you for your honest feedback. It improved the book tenfold. To our editors, Cat Woods and Kristin Donnan, and our graphic design maven, Alexis Clark, thank you for making the sound, look, and feel of the book top-notch. Because of your work, we are proud to have our book in the hands of professional educators everywhere. To our publisher, Rick Smith, thank you for not pulling any punches and pushing us to make the book simultaneously polished and accessible. Your feedback brought out the best in us and in the book. To our researcher, Amy Cosby-Frost, thank you for taking the appendix resources from good to great, so that they stand alone as a valuable resource.

And to our spouses, Paul Dearborn and Jen Sturgeon, who spent many weekends and evenings watching us sit at our computers, writing for hours on end, thank you for hanging in there through the last two years. You took up the slack with the family, rubbed our shoulders, reminded us to take breaks, read rough draft after rough draft, and loved us all the way through it. It would have been arduous to create this book without your support. We love you.

Finally, we would like to thank the countless compassionate and tireless teachers and administrators who over the years have inspired us with their dedication, commitment, and love for their most challenging students.

INTRODUCTION

> "Human behavior flows from three main sources: desire, emotion, and knowledge."
>
> — PLATO

Who We Are

From Grace

I have been in education for over 20 years, having started when I was in my early twenties. In that time I have held many positions, from classroom teacher to mentor teacher, from literacy coach to curriculum advisor. Currently I work as an independent consultant and instructional coach. The reason I started, and the reason I am still here, is because I love kids, especially teenagers. I love the wonder and the nonsense of working with adolescents. Call me crazy.

When I was in the classroom, I worked in some rough schools, primarily in the East Bay of the San Francisco Bay Area. I adored working with at-risk teens and their plethora of behaviors, the good, the bad, and the ugly. And the ugly was really ugly. I've had a stapler thrown at me, a chair thrown through my classroom window, and fistfights break out during class. I've had every curse word you can think of hurled at me by angry teens. Through all of this, the one thing I always had going for me was that I truly believed that anyone could be reached, connected with, and helped to grow academically and emotionally. It didn't even occur to me to question whether a 23-year-old, middle-class, white lady was the right person to teach 180 mostly Black and Hispanic teenagers, often from backgrounds of poverty and trauma. My naiveté and inexperience worked in my favor, though. I had no preconceived notions about how my students should behave or what they should be able to do. Because of this, I could

> "I love the wonder and the nonsense of working with adolescents."

meet them where they were and make plans to build from there, without resentment, disillusionment, or disappointment weighing me down.

In my early years, I got by mostly on enthusiasm, compassion, and a willingness to listen and learn. When it was clear that almost none of my students could read or write at a point even close to their grade level, I sought out support from others. The most effective tools I got for teaching writing came from a group of 4th- and 5th-grade teachers I met at a statewide conference. As I grew as a teacher, I learned from others how to make my learning environments safe and structured. I learned how to use incentives, relationships, and consequences to create clear expectations and to build trust and respect.

Effective educators are not born. They are grown. And they are ever changing. As we grow as educators, we are continually shaped by our experiences and by our interactions with key people and resources. If we are lucky, these people and resources will expand our understanding and our ability to meet the diverse needs of our students, especially our toughest. Scott Sturgeon, my co-author, was a key person in my growth. We hope this book will serve as a key resource in yours.

Food for Thought

Effective educators are not born. They are grown.

From Scott

I am a teacher. I have felt like a teacher for a long time, even before I held that title. I still think of myself as a teacher, and it has been over a decade since that was my primary job. I teach every day at work. Sometimes I teach kids, sometimes I teach adults, sometimes I teach my colleagues or my boss. Once you go into education, teaching is what you do.

I have seen some very successful kids, teachers, leaders, PTAs, and schools. Unfortunately, I have also seen educators and their students fail, both consistently and predictably. Predictable failure does not happen because of the demographic designation of a school, teacher, or student. Predictable failure happens when teachers or administrators let their egos, their personal issues, their ignorance, their mind-sets, or their biases get in the way of doing what is in the best interest of their students. And when educators fail, kids fail.

I am part of this book because I have seen adults and kids failing when I knew that it didn't have to be that way. I even might have had a hand in making sure it stopped being that way for some teachers and students. If so, I surely didn't do it alone; no one in education does. We look around for the people wiser and more experienced than we are, grab their best ideas and invite those ideas to live in our schools—where they can grow and change the lives of all who come there each day. My co-author, Grace Dearborn, is someone from whom I took many ideas and who helped people young and old to find success. Together, we changed the lives of some of our most vulnerable children and the people who care for them each day. Our hope is to help you do the same.

Straight Talk

When educators fail, kids fail.

Why We Wrote This Book

From Grace

As I travel around the country consulting at various schools, I continually have the following experience. I present a behavior-intervention workshop on "Conscious Classroom Management" to a group of teachers. Afterward, I'm approached by a teacher who says some version of the following: "I loved your presentation. It was so practical. I can't wait to try some things out. But, what about this kid?" Then I hear the story of a student with extreme, volatile, or dangerous behaviors with whom nothing has worked. I've answered this question many times, in many ways, depending upon the situation. Eventually it occurred to me that the answer to the question — "But, what about this kid?" — is something that is missing in current educational literature, training, and practice. At least, the practical answers, the actual solutions, are missing. I thought to myself, someone ought to write a book. I didn't think I would be that person. But then I met Scott Sturgeon.

Scott and I met when he hired my company, Conscious Teaching, to come to his school to do a series of classroom-management trainings. We worked with his staff as a whole, and also with a few specific teachers in one-on-one instructional coaching. He had taken over as principal at a school in distress in an urban, Midwestern school district—a low-performing school serving an impoverished area with an unusually large number of high-need kids. Scott was looking to drastically improve not only the academic achievement there, but also the school's climate and culture. The training I provided was well received, and Scott saw the potential for using it as a cornerstone piece in his plans for transforming the school. I spent several years collaborating with him and his staff. I helped him to help his staff shift their perceptions of, and interactions with, kids presenting with extreme behaviors in their classrooms. I was deeply impressed by how Scott interacted with and supported his teachers, how he worked with students who were sent to the office, and how he set up schoolwide and individual interventions to meet the extensive socio-emotional needs of his toughest kids. I know a lot about working with extreme student behaviors in a classroom, but I daresay Scott knows more. So I wondered, What if Scott and I put our heads together? Could we write the missing book? Turns out, we could. And we did. This is it.

From Scott

Sometimes teachers haven't witnessed the successes that Grace and I have seen and experienced. When you haven't seen success, hope becomes a rare commodity. I hope this book can make it a little less rare. I would like to think that you are going to find more than hope, though. You are going to find a path upon which a successful classroom or school can be built. Success in education is found all over the country, in every kind of school, with all types of challenges. Such successes share some common threads. This book is our attempt to make these threads visible and replicable.

Food for Thought

Success in education is found all over the country, in every kind of school, with all types of challenges.

We are going to leave the neurological and psychological explanations—of why and how kids do what they do—to the experts in those fields. What we will provide are the things that you can see, feel, hear, and try almost immediately. Don't let that mislead you into thinking that what we are advocating will be easy or quick to master. Like all good instructional techniques, the things we share in this book will take practice, time, patience, and hard work. If you give something a try, let us know how it went. If we can be of help, let us know. After all, we are teachers.

If your school has already invested time, energy, and resources in positive and preventative discipline structures, such as those found in our previous book, Conscious Classroom Management, 2nd Edition, then you probably have already seen a shift in campus climate and culture. You have likely seen a reduction in behavioral infractions and noticed improvement in teacher, student, and parent attitudes toward the school. But you also might still be struggling to meet the needs of a small percentage of students who present with extreme behaviors and with whom nothing seems to work. These students are often referred to as "frequent fliers," because they continue to be sent to the office, or continue to derail learning, almost daily, even after other schoolwide and classroom changes have found success with their peers. Positive structures and innovative teaching can take you only so far. Then what? We hope this book will answer that question and provide the missing pieces in your discipline and intervention puzzles, so you can help the most challenging kids in your school to find success.

Food for Thought

Positive structures and innovative teaching can take you only so far.

How We Know Success is Possible

From Grace

I have been consulting for Conscious Teaching (consciousteaching.com) in K-12 schools and districts around the country since 2010. I've worked with teachers in 44 of the 50 states, around classroom and schoolwide discipline and around student engagement, motivation, and intervention. I've worked rural to urban and poverty to affluent. I've seen both the amazing and the heart-breaking. And I have seen success happen in every type of school, regardless of location, demographics, or socio-economics. When both teachers and administrators are open, listening to one another, and making changes to better support the kids, magic happens. It happens everywhere in every kind of school. It really does. I've seen it. This book will hopefully provide you and your school with the resources necessary to begin the process of creating your own magic on your school site.

Food for Thought

When both teachers and administrators are open, listening to one another, and making changes to better support the kids, magic happens.

From Scott

When I was assigned as the principal at my second school, I had never worked with extreme poverty and with high referral rates. I had worked with students in self-contained behavior rooms for years and had served in behavioral support positions, but I had never spent time in a school like the one I was then assigned to, with all its wonder and challenges. In my first year at that school, I was working with approximately 500 students, 93% of whom were living in poverty. Reading scores were in the 50s and math scores were in the 30s. At the end of my first year there, we had 2000 referrals and 180 suspensions. At the end of my fourth year, our reading score was 78, our math score was 73; we had 650 referrals and 54 suspensions. That's nearly a 70% reduction in referrals and suspensions over three years.

I know that the approaches Grace and I share in this book work, because when faced with a daunting charge, my staff and I, with Grace's help, were able to work together to impressive success. We experienced firsthand what types of ideas, effort, and practice were instrumental in finding that success. We also draw upon similar, successful experiences from Grace's work all over the country, and not just with other elementary schools, but also with middle and high schools. We know you can find this kind of success too. And we are here to help.

How to Use This Book

This is not a book about diagnosing the causes of extreme behavioral problems in kids in schools. Plenty of other books out there thoroughly document the causes, from biological to environmental. Instead, our focus is on solutions. Teachers, administrators, and schools can take practical steps to meet the unique needs of these students. This book explains and gives examples of those practical steps.

The book is separated into three sections; Foundations, Interventions, and Leadership.

Section 1: Foundations	Section 2: Interventions	Section 3: Leadership
This section includes:	This section includes:	This section includes:
▲ Chapter 1: Identifying Tier 3 Kids	▲ Chapter 3: Classroom Discipline & Interventions	▲ Chapter 6: Leading the Change
▲ Chapter 2: Beliefs & Behaviors	▲ Chapter 4: Schoolwide Discipline & Interventions	▲ Chapter 7: A Plan for Change
	▲ Chapter 5: One-on-One Interventions	
The chapters in this section lay the foundation for working effectively with tough students. The focus is on the accurate identification of students requiring Tier 3 supports and the development of adult mind-sets and tools necessary to work with those students effectively.	The chapters in this section outline the practical techniques and structures we can use, both in the classroom and schoolwide, to better meet the needs of our toughest students. The focus is on the what, the how, and the where of effectively interacting with Tier 3 student behaviors.	The chapters in this section describe how administrators can support an entire staff through the change process. The focus is on building leadership skills and using those skills to generate staff buy-in, establish new structures, and create accountability for making necessary changes.

Ideally this book is meant for an entire staff, both teachers and administrators, to use together. Used in this way, it will have a profound impact. That's not to say, though, that it can't be used by individuals or smaller groups. It can.

You will get the most out of the book by reading it cover to cover. But if you are drowning and need something you can try tomorrow, feel free to jump right to the chapters that could fill your immediate need. We might suggest, for example:

- ▲ If you are a classroom teacher struggling with a disruptive student who is wreaking havoc in your classroom, then jump to Chapter 5.

- ▲ If you are an administrator looking for how to improve office discipline or how to have a conversation with staff about what needs to change, then jump to Chapter 6.

- ▲ If you are a teacher or support provider looking for de-escalation techniques to use with volatile or oppositional students, then jump to Chapter 4.

Whether you read the entire book or just one section, whether you read it on your own or with a team, you will walk away with practical techniques you can try immediately to support those students who need it the most.

Authors' Note About Pronoun Use:

Throughout the book, we use "they" and "their" as singular, gender-neutral pronouns in place of using "he" or "she." This was a conscious and purposeful choice on our part.

SECTION I —
Foundations

*Laying the Groundwork for Success
with Challenging Students*

1

IDENTIFYING TIER 3 KIDS

"All bad behavior is really a request for love, attention, or validation."

— KIMBERLY GILES,
HUMAN BEHAVIOR EXPERT

I N T H I S C H A P T E R, we define and explain what it means to be identified as a "Tier 3 kid." Tier 3 is a term commonly used in intervention programs to refer to children and teens who exhibit extreme behaviors in the classroom. It is essential to understand at the outset, however, that we do not use this label as either a moral judgment or a life sentence. From our perspective, being labeled Tier 3 does not consign a student to living within this definition for any specific length of time. It's only meant to identify the level of intervention and support they appear to need, based on their current actions and reactions in a classroom setting. In fact, when we are doing our jobs well, we identify these students more accurately, provide them with the supports they need, and help them to grow out of this label.

A Closer Look

Being labeled Tier 3 does not consign a student to living within this definition for any specific length of time.

▲ ▲ ▲

Who Tier 3 Kids Are—And Aren't

It isn't possible to predict or list every version of extreme behavior that might end with a student's being identified as needing Tier 3 support. Yet, all teachers and administrators can immediately name most of their Tier 3 students. These students are chronically disruptive, often volatile and oppositional, or are completely shut down. They aren't learning, and they often impede the ability of their peers to learn, as well. These "frequent fliers" rotate through the office on behavioral referrals weekly, daily, or hourly. They're the students who teachers and administrators cry over, lose sleep over, and tear their hair out over.

The term "Tier 3" comes from educational intervention programs initiated in the late 20th century that focused on meeting the diverse emotional and behavioral needs of students. Strategies for intervention with different students are chosen based on which behavioral tier a student falls into. You see this applied today in Positive Behavior Intervention & Support (PBIS), Response to Intervention (RTI), and similar intervention programs. This type of labeling is not inherently bad. The identification process allows us to make decisions about where to apply our limited energy and resources to best serve the unique needs of each child. Generally speaking, three tiers exist in a hierarchical triangle.

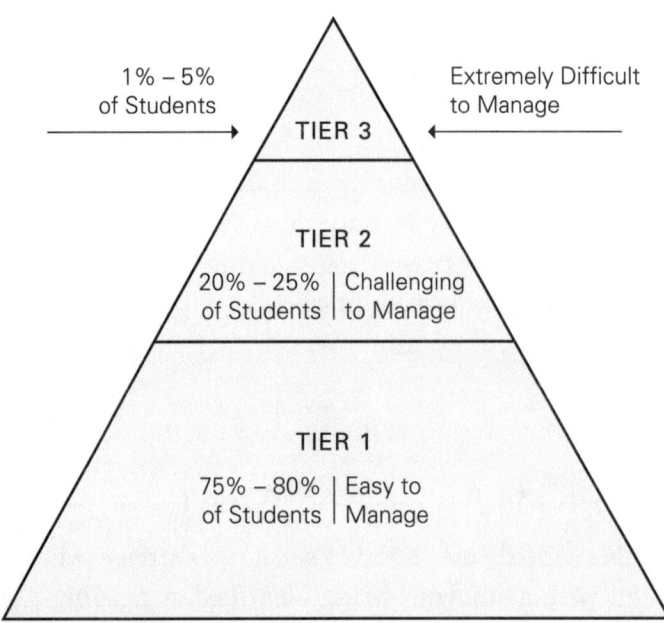

At the bottom is the largest tier, Tier 1. Students exhibiting Tier 1 behaviors are, for the most part, easy to manage in the classroom. They might mess around a bit, get off-task or occasionally disrupt, but the mildest interventions, consistently applied, will get them back on track. A verbal warning, a nonverbal directive, a stern look, or a quick, private conversation usually does the trick. Sometimes, a temporary seat change or phone call home might be required. But these interventions are not needed regularly—and when they are used, the child's behavior immediately improves for a significant amount of time before another infraction occurs, if one occurs at all. In an average school, students identified as Tier 1 make up about 75–80% of all students.

In the middle of the triangle is Tier 2, making up about 20–25% of all students. Students exhibiting Tier 2 behaviors require ongoing, consistent (daily or weekly) interventions to keep them focused and productive. The teacher might need to take special care in where they are seated and with whom they are grouped. To stay on task, these students might need extra reminders, visual cues, daily reinforcement, or small accommodations. Mild to moderate consequences need to be consistently and regularly applied to produce student cooperation with reasonable requests, but they do produce at least temporary cooperation. As compared with Tier 1, working with students who exhibit Tier 2 behaviors requires more time and energy. Still, while Tier 2 kids' off-task and disruptive behaviors can be tedious and draining, these students are manageable.

At the top of the triangle are students who exhibit Tier 3 behaviors. They make up about 1–5% of all students. Although they statistically represent a very small percentage of any student population, their behaviors are so extreme that they absorb the majority of a teacher's—and the administration's—time and energy. They disrupt learning and can be extremely volatile, oppositional, or defiant. Alternatively, they can shut down completely. No matter how calm, clear, and consistent the teacher is, no matter how compassionate and connected the teacher tries to be, and no matter what interventions or consequences are used or how they are applied, Tier 3 students do not alter their extreme behaviors significantly for any length of time.

Straight Talk

If you have identified more than 5% of your students as needing Tier 3 support, then you have almost certainly over-identified.

Over-Identification

If you have identified more than 5% of your students as needing Tier 3 support, then you have almost certainly over-identified. Statistically, an average American school will have 1–3% of its student population fall into Tier 3. In extreme cases, for schools in the highest poverty areas, or populations experiencing the highest amounts of toxic stress, that number might be as high as 4–5%.

From Scott

For four years, I was the principal at an elementary school where 93% of my students were receiving free and reduced lunch. The school had an unusually large number of students coming from backgrounds of extreme neglect, abuse, dysfunction, or gang-related activity. When I first took over this school, referrals, suspensions, and teacher recommendations caused more than 50 students (roughly 11%) to be identified as high need, or Tier 3. However, as we worked together as a staff to tighten our structures and get more purposeful, consistent, and compassionate with the application of our interventions and consequences, by the end of my second year only 21 students (roughly 5%) were informally classified as Tier 3.

Over-identification of Tier 3 students is incredibly common. Many students will exhibit outrageous behaviors that mimic Tier 3 behaviors, but these will abate when appropriate classroom and schoolwide structures are implemented with kindness and consistency.

So what is the difference between Tier 2 and Tier 3 students? A Tier 3 student is a student who, even when placed with the most effective teacher in the school, will regularly refuse to cooperate with the teacher or will routinely disrupt the learning of others by exploding or imploding. These behaviors don't change, even with appropriate use of traditional consequences and interventions that are consistently applied in the most skillful way possible. These students will harm themselves, academically and socially, in numerous ways that lead to head scratching and frustration on the part of the adults who care for them. By contrast, a Tier 2 student is a deeply shut-down or routinely disruptive student who, when placed with the most effective teacher in the school, responds positively, or shows some improvement in their behavior when appropriate traditional consequences or interventions are consistently and skillfully applied. Consequently, working effectively with extreme students starts with improving classroom structures and interactions, and supporting teachers in becoming the most calm, clear, connected, and consistent they can be. This also requires improving schoolwide systems and the way in which the administration supports the classroom teachers' efforts.

Moving Beyond Causes

Tier 3 behaviors have many possible causes, which generally fall into two categories: environmental or biological. Although this book's focus is not on underlying causes of Tier 3 behaviors, we often work more effectively with a student if we are aware of a cause. For example, if we know that the source of a student's extreme behavior is environmental, such as family or personal trauma or toxic stress, or we know it's biological, such as Fetal Alcohol Syndrome or lead poisoning, then we're more likely to respond from a place of empathy and compassion. In turn, we're more likely to stay on the child's side while working our way through a difficult intervention with them.

Food for Thought

Although it's best to try to unearth the cause of a student's extreme behaviors, this isn't necessary in order to work effectively with them.

Although it's best to try to unearth the cause of a student's extreme behaviors, this isn't necessary in order to work effectively with them. Whether or not we know the root causes, we usually can do little to nothing to alter them. We can't control a student's unstable, unhealthy, or unhappy home environment. We can't undo or reduce the number of Adverse Childhood Experiences (ACEs) they are struggling to overcome. We can't remove genetic, neurological challenges. As teachers, what we can control is how safe our classroom environments are and how we personally connect with these students. We can, through specific actions, help them learn trust, self-control, and emotional coping mechanisms. As administrators, we can control how we interact with these students when they are sent to the office and what schoolwide supports are in place to help them manage their big feelings and inappropriate actions. We can establish appropriate consequences, and enforce them from a place of love. We can thereby foster their understanding of where the boundaries are and how crossing boundaries leads to discomfort. We can personally connect with students, their families, and their teachers to let everyone involved know that we care, we are on their side, and growth is possible if we all work together.

When Adults Are Part of the Problem

Unfortunately, Tier 2 students are often misdiagnosed or mislabeled as Tier 3 students. This happens, in large part, when they're placed with inexperienced, ineffective, or struggling teachers. Tier 2 kids exhibit behaviors that are difficult yet manageable—but not when they find themselves in a chaotic or unsafe learning environment, overseen by a teacher who is overwhelmed or disconnected. Without suitable structures and support, Tier 2 students feel adrift. In a vacuum, without safety, structure, clarity, consistency, or reliable consequences, these students then spin out of control. Their otherwise manageable behaviors become unmanageable.

From Scott

In one school where I worked, I estimate that as much as 20% of the out-of-school student suspensions were adult created. A lack of appropriate supervision, calm reaction, or proper de-escalation dialogue led students to increase their self-injurious behavior. In each of these cases, the volatile or defensive adult reaction to a student's original outburst escalated the situation—ending in the student's taking additional actions that then necessitated suspension. A more deft adult response, delivered from a place of tenderness, would almost certainly have led to a more productive resolution.

We can't ignore the fact that teachers can and do take actions that sometimes escalate problems and increase volatile reactions from students. We also can't ignore the fact that administrators can and do take actions, or fail to act, in ways that undermine the behavioral learning of students and the authority of teachers. Chaos ensues and referrals and suspensions skyrocket when teachers and administrators are not at their best, lack the tools and training to work effectively with their toughest students and with each other, and are inconsistent, disconnected, or do not have simple, clear classroom and schoolwide systems in place designed to support behavioral learning.

Solutions & Possibilities

Solutions do exist. This book is about working effectively with Tier 3 students individually, in the classroom, and in the school as a whole. The situation in your classroom or school might be dire, but it isn't unsolvable. We will outline and give examples of successful techniques, systems, and interventions for classroom, administrative, and schoolwide use. These are the same solutions that Scott used in the Midwest, and that Grace used at a dozen more elementary and secondary schools across the country, where she worked or consulted.

Straight Talk

The situation in your classroom or school might be dire, but it isn't unsolvable.

Deep breath. Here we go...

2

BELIEFS &
BEHAVIORS

*"Engrave this upon your heart:
there isn't anyone you couldn't
love once you heard their story."*

— MARY LOU KOWNACKI, BENEDICTINE NUN
& NON-VIOLENCE EDUCATOR

I N THIS CHAPTER, we discuss how our assumptions and beliefs about students with challenging behaviors determine how we interact with them, for better or for worse. When we harbor negative feelings about students who chronically act out, we unconsciously give them less respect, patience, and flexibility than we give our other students. This adds fuel to the fire that is their misbehavior, ensuring that it continues to grow, rather than being managed or extinguished. In this chapter, we offer some simple, practical techniques that can break this negative cycle of interaction. When adults use these techniques, they can see the best in their students and hold them gently in their hearts — even when it's necessary to give consequences for misbehavior.

▲　▲　▲

Perception Creates Reality

A classic tale: A traveler heading north comes to a fork in the road, where the path heading east leads to a nearby town. He greets a food seller who has set up a table there, asking what the people are like in the town. The food seller asks the traveler, "What were the people like in the town you came from?" The traveler replies, "They were awful. Selfish and mean." The food seller responds, "The people in this town are exactly the same." The traveler thanks the food seller and continues straight on, seeking a better town to stop in. A little while later, another traveler heading north passes by and stops to ask the food seller what the

Food for Thought

Perception determines reality.

people are like in the nearby town. As before, the food seller asks this new traveler what the people were like in the town they came from. The new traveler replies, "They were wonderful! Generous and friendly." The food seller responds, "The people in this town are exactly the same." The traveler thanks the food seller and heads east, toward the town.

The moral of this story is that perception determines reality. For everyone involved.

If you make assumptions about other people, then you are human. If you make negative assumptions about students, and then rely on those assumptions to make decisions about them, then you are doomed.

The Covenant of Care

Excerpted from *Conscious Classroom Management,*
2nd Edition, by Rick Smith and Grace Dearborn

In our previous book, *Conscious Classroom Management,* we wrote that safety and structure are the two pillars of effective classroom management. Our students want both, even if their behavior seems to scream the opposite. There is an invisible covenant between teachers and students. This "covenant of care" forms the foundation of successfully working with Tier 3 students.

The student's covenant says:

"Please teach me appropriate behavior in a safe and structured environment. I may act out, I may behave in ways that suggest I don't care, but in truth I really do. I want to learn appropriate behavior, and I won't be satisfied unless you are holding your ground, teaching this to me."

The teacher's covenant says:

"I will do my best to teach you appropriate behavior in a safe and structured environment. I will assume that you want to learn this. I will not give up on you or stop caring about you, no matter what evidence you may demonstrate to the contrary."

As teachers, the beliefs we hold, the motivations we assign, and the judgments we make about all kids—especially our toughest— determine how we interact with them and whether or not we can ultimately help them. If we assume that our most difficult students want positive attention, love, and respect, then we will perceive their negative behaviors as cries for help. We will see their misbehavior as stemming from trauma, neglect, or disability. We will feel compassion for them and work hard to find ways to help them. On the other hand, if we assume that our most difficult students don't care or are bad kids, then we will deem them as less worthy of our time, care, and attention. We will perceive their negative behaviors as a personal attack and will punish them for being disrespectful. The thing is, there is no absolute "truth." We have only perception to rely upon. What we choose to believe about our students is the lens through which we perceive them. Our perception determines our reality, and our reality determines our actions.

Kids & Why They Act Out

Kids who act out at school or resist learning are not "bad kids." We can identify dozens of reasons why kids might act out in class, even if we remove the "special circumstances," or underlying life causes of Tier 3 behaviors. You've probably seen them all; some of the most common reasons include:

- ▲ Tired
- ▲ Bored
- ▲ Hungry
- ▲ Anxious
- ▲ Traumatized
- ▲ Overwhelmed
- ▲ Need Attention
- ▲ Attention-Deficit
- ▲ Low Self-Esteem
- ▲ Low Impulse Control
- ▲ Low Academic Ability
- ▲ Emotionally Disturbed

A Closer Look

If we assume that our most difficult students want positive attention, love, and respect, then we will perceive their negative behaviors as cries for help.

You might consider and manage a hungry kid's outburst differently from an outburst by a kid with low academic ability—one needs a sandwich; the other might never be able to master today's topic in class. Understanding what you are working with informs your intervention. But regardless of why a student is acting out, it's always—always—more effective for us to choose to assume the best about them. And no matter what they say, they do care. Kids who act out don't do it because they want to. They do it because they don't know how else to feel in control. However, although these kinds of behavioral coping mechanisms can help them to feel a modicum of control over their lives, the same mechanisms often conflict with what's best for them in school and in life.

Bright Idea

Regardless of why a student is acting out, choose to assume the best about them.

Kids whose lives feel out of control will grab control wherever they can find it. Some grab eating. Some grab academic excellence. Some grab acting out. Children who develop eating disorders have been found, at least in part, to be trying to exert control over their lives in the one place they can—choosing to eat or not to eat. Nobody thinks they're bad kids or that they don't care about their own health and happiness. On the other hand, kids with behavior issues in school are often categorized as not caring or bad. Once we've labeled them in this way, we can rationalize away our guilt for giving up on them or not being able to reach them. "It's their fault, not ours." Once we change that thinking, we have more chance of success.

Our Unspoken Intention

As educators, we often enter the profession hoping that we can change the world, or at least the worlds of our students. Maybe we seek to save kids, or give them the same wonderful experience we had as students. Or, maybe we seek to ensure the opposite of what we experienced, in order to reach students—who, like ourselves, were once unreachable. Armed with this toolkit of purpose and a bellyful of care, we enter the field of education. We are then immediately assaulted by the extreme behaviors of some of our most traumatized students. We are initially stunned, then frustrated, then defensive, then angry. We start to question the motivations of these students. Our commitment to the "covenant of care" begins to falter. Then we hear a student's history of abuse or trauma and our hearts break open.

The horrific must not allow us to empathize ourselves out of our expectations or accountability for our students. Nor can our expectations allow us to cut students out of our hearts. We have to find the middle road, the balance between being firm and soft. Most importantly, we have to communicate to them that we will be there for them, no matter what choices they make.

This communication cannot just be verbal. More important than the things we say are the things we do that express our **unspoken intention**. Students see our unspoken intention on our faces and in our posture, and they hear it in our tone. Regardless of what words we use, they understand our intention by these cues, and they respond to that more than to our words. This is part of the reason why some teachers can tell an oppositional student to step outside — and then successfully resolve a volatile situation — while other teachers cannot. Even though both teachers might give the same consequence and say the same words, the student will respond to differences in their unspoken intentions.

A Closer Look

Students see our unspoken intention on our faces and in our posture, and they hear it in our tone.

To be clear, though, believing the best about students and staying on their side does not mean that we let them slide. We must continually hold them accountable for their unproductive behavioral choices. Even consequences for major disruptions and defiance can be given from a place of internal empathy, or positive unspoken intention, while remaining completely firm and consistent. It's the difference between giving a consequence to help a student learn to make better choices — and to see us as someone who cares — versus giving a consequence to punish them for making our lives a little harder (see chart on page 35).

Although the consequence we use might be identical, the quality of the interaction is likely very different because our unspoken intention is different. Ultimately, kids pick up on quality more than anything else.

Holding challenging students accountable for their unproductive behaviors and choices in a compassionate way is easier said than done. In Chapter 3 we outline how to express positive intention through various non-verbal cues while redirecting misbehavior. Meanwhile, the following section presents a technique for finding and holding positive intention within yourself, especially in tough moments with kids.

The Invisible Subtitle

Imagine that each of your students has an invisible subtitle running along in front of them. The purpose of this subtitle is to communicate to you, and any other adults in their lives, what they really need when they act out or shut down. Everything else — the complaints and resistance that come out of their mouths and bodies during these difficult interactions — is just noise. It's just the interference we need to look beyond in order to see, read, and respond to their subtitle.

Bright Idea

Imagine that each of your students has an invisible subtitle running along in front of them that is communicating to you what they really need.

As much as possible, try to ignore the noise and respond to the subtitle. For example, the subtitle might say, "This is hard for me. Help me to succeed, and let me save face, too." As teachers, if we can decipher each subtitle — instead of losing our cool, raising our voices, and lecturing students about disrespect and appropriate language — then we can respond more compassionately and more productively. We might say, "Yes. I know this is hard, and sometimes hard things feel unnecessary and we want to avoid them. But I'm here to help. Let's work on it together." The student replies, "No. I don't want your help. I can't do this." We might respond, "I get it. This is hard. I'm going to help you."

Positive Unspoken Intention	Negative Unspoken Intention
Motivation: To meet the student's need for safety and structure, to communicate and reinforce clear boundaries, and to build mutual respect.	*Motivation:* To meet the teacher's need for order and control, to communicate and reinforce clear boundaries, and to establish dominance.
Consequence: Temporary change of seat	*Consequence:* Temporary change of seat
Teacher uses consequences supportively, to teach appropriate behavior. This unspoken intention is communicated in the following ways:	Teacher uses consequences reactively, to punish, humiliate, or save face. This unspoken intention is communicated in the following ways:

Positive Unspoken Intention	Negative Unspoken Intention
▲ Facial expression shows concern.	▲ Facial expression shows frustration or anger.
▲ Body language is relaxed, but firm.	▲ Body language is either threatening or fearful.
▲ Voice is quiet and compassionate.	▲ Voice is loud and either hostile or pleading.
▲ Attitude is genuine and sincere.	▲ Attitude is sarcastic, dismissive, or exasperated.
▲ Words are few, clear, and supportive: "Move to the back for a minute and try to regain your focus."	▲ Words are unclear, blaming, and aggressive: "That's enough! I have told you four times to stop doing that. What is the matter with you? Go to the back and stay there until you're ready to show some respect."

Behavioral subtitles are ours to decipher. They are written in the language of children and teens who are not mature or skilled enough to express in words how unsafe they feel in the world. These kids aren't capable of appropriately processing their feelings of frustration, inadequacy, fear, or anger. They are communicating through their actions instead, and it's the adults' job to figure out what they mean — and decide how best to respond.

From Grace

I've often been caught off guard by a student's outburst or resistance. When that happens, it's harder for me to stay calm enough to remember to look for the subtitle, especially if I feel personally attacked. In these situations, when I don't have the time or energy to figure out what their invisible subtitle might be, I will throw in a default subtitle. Usually I use, "Please help me," or "Don't give up on me." Either of these helps me to stay calm and respond productively to misbehavior, instead of unintentionally escalating or creating a confrontation. I can only do this, though, if I can hold onto the belief or assumption that student outbursts are tests that they want me to pass, or cries for help, and not disrespect.

Assuming the best and finding the invisible subtitle isn't about being permissive or about ignoring unproductive and disruptive behaviors. It's about understanding that misbehavior is a request for help, and not a personal attack. If we assume that kids want to be appropriate, then when they aren't we can assume it's their way of saying, "I don't know how to be appropriate in this situation, and I need you to teach me." Or, "I know I'm being inappropriate, but I'm doing it to test you, to see if you care enough about me to hold me accountable for better behavior in a firm but kind way." Or, "I know I'm being inappropriate, but I'm so triggered I feel like I can't control it or stop. Please hold me accountable, but also please keep me safe and don't give up on me." In other words, we perceive their misbehavior as their way of communicating to us the following types of questions:

Bright Idea

Have a default subtitle you can always hear in your head when volatile situations arise unexpectedly. For example, you might choose to hear, "Help me" or "Please don't give up on me".

▲ How much do you really care about me?

▲ How far can I push you before you lash out at me or start ignoring me?

▲ Do you care enough about me to do the hard work of putting your personal issues aside and teaching me to be appropriate?

▲ Can you hold me accountable for my behavior in a totally firm yet completely loving way, even when I act like I don't care or don't want to learn?

Straight Talk

Student outbursts are cries for help, not disrespect.

When we are able to look past their misbehavior to the subtitle beyond, the delivery of our consequences and other interventions is softened by compassion and empathy. Our unspoken intention shifts from wanting to punish to wanting to support. But we still deliver consequences.

Responding to Student Resistance

Here are some common examples of student behavior, the subtitles that might be attached, and how we can respond to them, while assuming the best about the student and their motivations:

What Students Say	What Students Mean (Subtitles)	How Teachers Can Respond
This is stupid / boring. (OR) I can't / won't do this.	This is hard. Please help me.	**Yep. This stuff is hard. Let me help you.**
Teacher: What you just said/did isn't okay. You cannot do/say that in class. Student: **I don't care.**	I do care. In fact, I care a lot. But I can't tell you that. Please don't be disappointed in me. Show me that you care.	**Ok, but I care. It's not okay with me that you aren't being your best self. So let's do this....**

What Students Say	What Students Mean (Subtitles)	How Teachers Can Respond
Teacher: Good morning. Student: **Whatever.** (Rolls eyes.)	I don't feel good this morning. I doubt anyone cares.	**Are you okay? Can I help you in some way?**
Teacher: Sit down. Student: (Grumbles loudly, knocks another student's books on floor while walking to desk, slumps into chair.)	I'm frustrated and feeling bad, and now you're mad at me, too. I can't do anything right.	**Come talk with me a moment. Are you okay? Let's fix what just happened.**
Teacher: (Teacher begins a lesson, introducing new topic or content.) Student: **Why do we have to do this? When will I ever need to know/use this?**	I have a lot of demands on my time and energy, and a lot of work we do in school seems irrelevant to me. Please help me see the relevance in what you're asking me to do right now, so I can feel motivated to try.	**You're right that you might never need to know this exact information. But any time you try something that's new or hard for you, your brain grows and gets heavier. Heavy brains are smart brains. Smart brains belong to people who get good jobs and have the lives they want. So we're doing this so you can grow a heavy brain and someday have the life you want.**
Teacher: Stop talking. Student: **What!? I'm not talking!** (OR) **Why are you picking on me! Everyone is talking!**	I know I was talking, but I can't admit it. If you leave me alone now, I'll try to stop and pay attention. (OR) I know I'm talking. But it feels unfair that I get called out and nobody else does.	**Perfect. Moving on.** (OR) **You're right. Others are talking. So you focus on you, and then I will focus on others.**

What Students Say	What Students Mean (Subtitles)	How Teachers Can Respond
Teacher: Pick up your pencil and begin the assignment. Student: (Ignores teacher and does nothing.)	I'm too tired / depressed / stressed to do what you're asking. My life is in disarray, and nobody will help me.	**Are you feeling okay? Do you need to see the nurse? How can I help you? How about you get a drink of water or take a breath outside, and then we will figure out how I can help.**

Teacher Failure

When we try all year, but are not able to reach or help a particular student, that isn't failure. Failure is when we stop caring about that student and stop trying to help. All challenging students will push our buttons at some point. But the ones who have us by our last nerve are the ones who most need us not to give up on them.

Kids don't act out in a vacuum. Most of the time, students who present with the most difficult personalities and behavioral choices in the classroom have learned through experience that adults cannot be trusted to keep them safe. Still, deep down, they hope for an exception. They hope that an adult will treat them with respect, hold them firmly but gently accountable, and never give up, no matter what awful things they do or say. So they test us by acting out in class. They are trying to find out if we can teach them where the boundaries are between acceptable, encouraged, and forbidden—without lashing out at them. Or giving up on them. Some kids test us subtly and quietly. Some run full speed into the abyss, seeking to find the edge. Either way, they are collecting evidence, watching, and noting how we respond.

Straight Talk

Failure isn't when we can't reach a student. Failure is when we stop trying to reach them.

Let's say we pass the first test. We redirect their behavior in a calm, safe, and structured way. Rest assured, the testing isn't over — and usually, it gets worse before it gets better. Tier 3 kids are familiar with having their hopes dashed; they know disappointment, abuse, and abandonment. Therefore, the better we do at passing their tests, the more vulnerable they feel. Almost against their will, they start to trust us. Just a little. Then they get nervous. They worry that ultimately we will still give up on them down the road. In their experience, this is inevitable, and their hurt will be that much more devastating. So they act out even more, worse than before. They have to break us before we break them. Usually, they do.

> *"The hurt that troubled children create*
> *is never greater than the hurt they feel."*
>
> — L. TOBIN, YOUTH ADVOCATE & AUTHOR

We're only human. It's easy to forget — even discard — the idea that Tier 3 students want to learn and be loved. It's easy to feel powerless in the face of a protracted onslaught of negative behaviors that get worse over time — no matter what consequences we use, no matter how calm, clear, and kind we are in the process, and no matter how consistently proactive and positive we try to be. It's easy to eventually give up.

In the worst-case scenario, we might have invested huge amounts of energy into our most challenging students, without "getting anything back" from them. We might get so exasperated that we throw up our hands and conclude, "This one can't be reached," or "That one has to meet me halfway," or "I've done what I can do," or "I led them to water, but it's up to them to drink." All of these responses are the equivalent of giving up, of emotional abandonment. And students know it. Maybe we still go through the motions with them, but our hearts aren't in it. We no longer believe they can change, or even that they want to. We just bide our time until the year ends, when they will become somebody else's problem. We accept our fate as a number, just another statistic in their growing body of evidence against adults.

From Grace

When I am at a standstill with a student, I try to cut myself a break. My mission is to keep the metaphorical door open for them—both emotionally and educationally—and to continually encourage them to walk through it, in my speech, actions, and attitude toward them. If they don't walk through the door, that's okay. Kids make their own choices. I can't force them through the door, but I can make it more uncomfortable to resist walking through than to comply. In the end, failure for me wasn't when one of my students didn't succeed or didn't change behaviorally. Failure for me was when I stopped trying, when I stopped caring if a student walked through the door, and when I communicated to them in speech or action that I was "done." I've failed in this way more than once. But over time, as I reflected on these failures, sought out support from others, and began experimenting with different ways of being and acting when similar situations arose, these types of failures occurred less and less.

In my fifth year of teaching high school, I experienced for the first time the dramatic impact that not giving up on a kid can yield. A difficult student from the year before came by my room for a visit. We chatted for a few minutes and then he said, "You know, you're a really good teacher. You're the best teacher I ever had." I was speechless. This was a student who had been consistently confrontational, abrasive, off-task, and inappropriate in my class. Despite my best efforts, he hadn't ever shown the slightest improvement in his behavior or his academic skills. He had failed my course and repeated it in summer school. How could I possibly be, in his eyes, a "good teacher?" This is when I first started to really understand that a lack of change on the outside doesn't mean a student isn't changing on the inside—and that we should never give up. Ever. Not on them, and not on ourselves. We truly never know how we are internally affecting our toughest students.

Food for Thought

Lack of change on the outside doesn't mean a student isn't changing on the inside.

Three Questions

Ask yourself the following three questions:

1. Do I honestly believe it's my job to help my most difficult students to improve their behavior?

2. Do I honestly believe I'm capable of helping my most difficult students to improve their behavior, even if the other adults in their lives are not helping me, or them?

3. Do I honestly believe that my most difficult students want to improve their behavior?

If you didn't answer a firm and unequivocal "YES" to all three of these questions, then you will probably struggle to work effectively with Tier 3 students. If you don't believe it's your job, that you are capable of it, and the kids want to learn it, then you won't put 100% of yourself behind the techniques and systems that could help you. Consequently, you will unconsciously undermine the process by implementing new techniques half-heartedly, or for too short a period of time, and you'll be ready for them to fail. You'll always be looking for evidence that these techniques are not working—rather than for evidence that they are—to feed your underlying belief that change isn't possible or that it isn't your job to manifest it.

Our experience has been that the best behavioral outcomes with Tier 3 kids begin from honestly answering "yes" to these three questions. However, if right now you would answer "no" to one or more of them, don't give up hope. There are many valid reasons for answering "no." Perhaps you once would have answered "yes," but lost faith after years of working in under-resourced or poorly managed schools. Perhaps you are struggling with your own personal history of trauma or toxic stress, and it's too much to take on someone else's. Perhaps you think it's impossible to succeed with certain students without the right kind of support from your administration or colleagues. Perhaps you never thought about these types of questions before, and are skeptical that they are part of the job you thought you signed up for. Perhaps you just need to see it work, before you can believe it will work. Whatever might be holding you back from "yes," if you are willing to leave the door of possibility open, willing to have conversations with your peers in an open forum, and willing to experiment with new ways of interacting with your Tier 3 kids, then you just might find success anyway.

Intervention, Not Revenge

If you are frustrated with the daily necessity of dealing with negative student behaviors, then you are firmly in the center of the average teacher's experience. Managing difficult student behaviors will eventually run down almost any teacher, no matter how talented or experienced.

When we become overwhelmed by the magnitude or frequency of the misbehaviors we have to deal with, the danger increases that our interactions with difficult students will shift from a focus on prevention to a focus on revenge. Our unspoken intention turns toward vengeance, we become blind to their invisible subtitles, and we lash out in frustration. Instead of preventing an escalation, we cause it. Instead of preventing future outbursts, we inadvertently encourage them. Our learning environment becomes unsafe, our relationship with our students degrades, we dread coming to work, and we lay the blame at the feet of the kids. When this happens, the first step in righting the ship is getting back in touch with our positive assumptions about our toughest kids. We can lean on the techniques in this chapter to help us. But this is only the first step. We need more than just positive assumptions to create productive change. We also need practical techniques.

The chapters coming up in Section II of this book are chock-full of take-away techniques and practical recommendations for working with our most difficult students. However, each of these techniques depends on starting from a place of belief—belief in ourselves and in our ability to help, belief in our students

Straight Talk

If you don't believe teaching behavioral lessons is your job, that you are capable of it, and that all your students want to learn it, then you will unconsciously undermine the process.

and in their desire to be different and better, and belief in possibilities yet unseen. Without these foundational beliefs in place, we are unlikely to make a significant difference.

A Closer Look

Focus on prevention, not revenge.

▲ ▲ ▲

Yeah Buts & What Ifs....

Teacher: But don't they have to meet me halfway?

No, they don't. That isn't their job. Their job is to survive, to try to keep themselves physically, emotionally, and psychologically safe in any way they can. Unfortunately, sometimes the things they do in an effort to achieve that safety appear to us to be negative, weird, unhelpful, disrespectful, or oppositional. They build a moat between us and them, for security. They fill it with outrageous and unproductive behaviors as a defense. It's our job to reach out across that murky chasm to where they are, and encourage them to come toward us. When they don't, it's our job to get creative and find new and different ways to encourage them. Build ladders, rope swings, bridges, helicopters, catapults, human cannons. When we build these things and they still refuse to budge, it's our job to be patient and keep reaching out by making it clear in our words and actions that we want them to come across to us. If they let us, then we will be there to walk or fly or hop or swing with them. If they still refuse, then it's our job to love them from afar and always leave the possibility open, even if they choose never to come across.

Teacher: But I shouldn't be working harder than them, right?

You aren't. If we assume the best about them, then we can assume that their difficult and resistant behaviors stem from internal feelings that are pulling them apart and requiring them to find ways—even unproductive ways—to protect themselves from psychologically disintegrating. Creating mental and emotional armor to protect oneself from what is perceived to be an unkind, uncaring, or dangerous world takes a tremendous amount of effort to both build and sustain. These kids are working hard at it. Harder than you are at trying to prove that you care, that your classroom is safe, that there are other more productive ways to be in the world, and that they don't need to wear that armor around you.

However, let's suppose, for the sake of argument, that you are working harder than they are. You can and you should. That's literally what you're being paid to do. This isn't college. They aren't here by choice. You are. They aren't choosing to spend their days at school. You are. They aren't invested in being awesome at what they do at school. You are. They can't be fired for a job poorly done. You can. If we ever hope to have any success with our most challenging students, then we have to get past our own excuses and rationalizations. We have to stop blaming the kids, the parents, the community, or society. We have to make peace with the fact that for them we will work harder than we want to, harder than we will for our other students, and maybe, occasionally, even harder than they're working. That's okay, because that's the job.

Straight Talk

Kids aren't in school by choice. Teachers are.

Administrator: But what if most of my teachers answered "no" to one or more of the "Three Questions"?

First, don't be surprised. This will, most likely, happen to you. Second, if you work at a school with a history of behavioral challenges, then all teacher responses provide important data points to inform your work. If you are going to change the way student behavior is viewed, approached, and reacted to, then you must know where your staff stands. Third, you, the administrator, have to be ready to hear and use critical feedback to make your own changes—and to support your teachers. Ultimately, you set the tone and lead the way. If you aren't walking the walk yourself—of reflecting, experimenting, and trying new things to support both your Tier 3 students and your reluctant teachers—then your teachers likely won't listen to you. If you aren't taking risks and challenging yourself, if you aren't experimenting outside your own comfort zone, then you can't expect your teachers to.

> **A Closer Look**
>
> "Kind and constructive" should be the tone of any conversation about change.

However, you can't wait until your entire staff changes their answers to "yes" for change to begin. You can start by gently challenging anyone who is holding back, doubtful, or afraid. Here are some ways to begin:

1. At a staff meeting, run a Socratic seminar or a friendly debate about each of the three questions. Challenge folks to defend their positions, and listen carefully to both positive and negative answers. Although some teachers might have legitimate reasons to answer "no" to these questions, their resistance can't end the debate. Acknowledge and empathize with someone's personal truth or past experience, and then address their concerns. For some resources that might help you with this, see Appendix E. Also, don't let negative voices overshadow positive ones. Ask people to communicate from a place of empathy for students and families. "Kind and constructive" should be the tone of any conversation about change.

2. Implement a plan that includes discussion, explanation, and training. For some educators, this will be enough to bring them closer to the "yes"; for others, it won't. Even without 100% buy-in, go ahead and change the building's expectations and discipline systems to align with your beliefs about how best to support kids. Communicate

those expectations and systems clearly to all staff, and hold all staff accountable for acting in alignment with them, whether they believe in them or not. Some people need to see something work before they'll believe it can work.

3. Even hesitant teachers can agree that if they keep doing what they're doing, they'll keep getting what they're getting. Try framing your new mindset, or way of being, or technique as an "experiment." Even if some people can't answer "yes" to one or more of the questions, they can still try out new ideas and strategies to see if they work.

Administrator: But my teachers already think I'm being too soft. Won't that perception worsen when I ask them to take on these assumptions, or answer "YES" to the "Three Questions"?

Anything short of a suspension makes some teachers think their principal is soft. Therefore, seeing you in action is the only real solution to any misperceptions your staff might have about your strengths, weaknesses, or discipline style. It's also how they learn the school's policies—including the teacher's role in discipline and intervention.

Seeing you in action requires dialogue—dialogue about difficult kids, discipline systems, mindsets, and assumptions. These conversations are two-way streets, and it's important to remember that "listening" is not the same thing as "being soft." By hearing honest feedback—about policies, as well as your approach—you can begin to address concerns. However, you are the leader. It's up to you to process the information you receive, and make decisions. There's nothing "soft" about that.

Administrator: But what can I do with critical feedback from my teachers about how my team and I handle discipline?

1. When concerns are valid, then you can apologize. If your teachers have picked out instances where you or your team

didn't handle a discipline situation effectively, you can acknowledge that it should have been handled differently. You can commit to doing better, without promising to be perfect.

A Closer Look

Seeing you in action is the only real solution to any misperceptions your staff might have about your strengths, weaknesses, or discipline style.

2. When concerns are based on partial information, then you must make a judgment call. For example, you might have made a decision about a kid or a situation based on details that teachers weren't privy to. Decide what information is appropriate to share — and at least explain that there were extenuating circumstances. In these cases, circumstances might prevent teachers from understanding a particular decision, but the more transparent you can be, the better. When teachers understand how you operate, they're more likely to perceive you as competent and on their side.

3. When concerns are not valid or realistic, then you can gently challenge them. That's another part of being a leader.

If you want your staff to perceive you as strong and supportive, then you must: hear their grievances without being defensive; take responsibility for where you've fallen short; brainstorm about what changes they would like to see made at the administrative level; hash out which of their requests are realistic; and then follow through by doing at least one or two things differently. Then perceptions will start to shift.

▲ ▲ ▲

Summary & Applications

Remember

- ▲ All misbehavior can be perceived as disrespect or as a request for help. You get to choose how you want to perceive it.

- ▲ Our "Unspoken Intention" speaks louder than our words when we are in disciplinary situations with students. Intending to support is always more effective than intending to punish.

- ▲ Be prepared for students to test you by misbehaving or not cooperating. Remind yourself that this is normal and not personal. It's just how kids determine whether you are safe, structured, and caring enough to hold them gently but firmly accountable for appropriate behavior and effort.

- ▲ Don't give up on kids whose behavior doesn't change over time. Remind yourself that kids change internally before they change externally. Be patient. Believe in the process even when there isn't yet any external evidence to support it.

Discuss

- ▲ What is the thing that students say or do that really pushes your buttons? If you assume the best about the student, what's a possible "Invisible Subtitle" for that thing? How might you respond more productively to this situation in the future?

- ▲ Think of a time when you mishandled or accidently escalated a volatile situation with a challenging student. What was your "Unspoken Intention"? If you could go back in time, how might you have handled it differently?

- ▲ What kinds of "testing" do you usually come up against with students at the beginning of the year? How might you prepare to pass these tests more effectively in the future?

Apply

▲ Create a list of student behaviors that cause you to feel frustrated. Then list, or discuss with a colleague, one or two possible "Invisible Subtitles" for each behavior on your list.

▲ Role-play with friends or colleagues the most common things kids say to you that push your buttons or make you feel attacked, angry, or frustrated. Practice reading and responding to the possible subtitles in each situation. Focus on being clear, calm, and kind, without letting the student off the hook.

▲ Discuss the "Three Questions." If you answered "no" to any of them, consider what it would take to move you to a tentative "yes." Plan to take an active step in that direction—no matter how small—just to see what happens.

SECTION II —
Interventions

*Meeting the Specific Needs
of Challenging Students*

3

CLASSROOM DISCIPLINE

EFFECTIVE DISCIPLINE AND INTERVENTION, isn't just about what we do, it's also about who we are and how we do it. In this chapter, we will look at the three distinct but interlinked elements that determine whether or not classroom discipline is effective: The Teacher, The Tools, and The Process. We will start by exploring the characteristics of several different types of teachers and how their individual characteristics help or hinder disciplinary efforts in the classroom. Then we will look at the practical tools that can be used to intervene effectively with student misbehavior during class. And finally we will look at the process, or how we can use these tools to produce the best possible outcomes, for us and for our Tier 2 and Tier 3 students.

However, we will not be looking at positive discipline structures or preventative measures that would be used more commonly at Tier 1. This book focuses generally — and this chapter specifically — on what to do when those positive and preventative techniques have taken you as far as you can go, yet you still struggle with certain students who continue to be difficult, disruptive, defiant, or shut down. For a comprehensive resource on Tier 1 and Tier 2 interventions, check out Conscious Classroom Management, 2nd Edition, by Rick Smith and Grace Dearborn.

▲ ▲ ▲

PART 1: THE TEACHER

Classrooms are populated by people — and people are unique. We all find different ways of adapting to our surroundings and trying to get our individual needs met. Our most challenging students do this in a myriad of ways that often undermine their learning. In response, we — the teachers — apply various interventions in an attempt to better support them. Sometimes, these interventions lead to greater success for both the students and for us. And sometimes, they do not. Even when we're using "tried and true," research-based methods, success depends largely on how we perceive our resistant students and how we interact with them, both verbally and non-verbally.

Teachers & What Doesn't Work

As we consult across the country, we see certain themes that come up over and over with teachers who are struggling to work effectively with kids displaying Tier 3 behaviors. Over time, we've identified two types of teachers who tend to struggle the most. You might see yourself or some of your colleagues in these descriptions, but these descriptions are not judgments. The first step in working more effectively with kids is looking honestly at ourselves and identifying what we are doing that isn't working. From there, we can attempt strategic changes that might benefit everyone.

Straight Talk

The first step in working more effectively with kids is looking honestly at ourselves and identifying what we are doing that isn't working.

The two types of teachers we identified are permissive teachers and authoritarian teachers. The permissive type allows too much misbehavior to go on unchecked before intervening, if they intervene at all. The authoritarian type unintentionally creates or escalates confrontations with kids. Both of these types of teachers are missing balance in their approaches. They haven't yet found the sweet spot, where structure meets the open heart.

There is a third type of teacher who struggles, as well, but for a very different reason. This is the balanced teacher who lacks adequate outside support. Balanced teachers have the skill to deal effectively with most behaviors in the classroom—but on rare occasions when they need outside support from the school or administration, they are not getting it. We talk at length about the need for, and the issues around, schoolwide and administrative support in Chapter 4. Therefore, for this chapter, let's focus on the overly permissive teacher and the overly authoritarian teacher, and how their disciplinary choices sometimes exacerbate classroom problems. Then we will look at the concrete steps that can be taken to move toward a more balanced and effective approach.

The Permissive Teacher

Permissive teachers are often defined by having their hearts on their sleeves. These teachers scream empathy—or more often, sympathy—for their students. They know the entire life histories of their students, especially the hard cases who have had little success in any other classroom. They believe that when challenging students enter their rooms, love can solve any and all problems.

The strength of the permissive teacher is that they often have, or attempt to have, strong relationships with students and their families. However, they also have weak boundaries. A sad story accompanies every issue brought to the permissive teacher's attention. "Johnny only does that because...." They regularly offer rewards, prizes, and out-of-school relationship-building to bring that hard-case student around. What they lack is a consistent way of addressing the student in a manner that defines clear expectations and firm boundaries. If the student continues to act out—which means that the teacher's attempt at loving the student into behaving has failed—then the teacher often snaps.

A Closer Look

The permissive teacher has a relationship, but little structure.

The result is that a familiar, ongoing, previously ignored student behavior—unaddressed for hours, days, or weeks—suddenly sparks a referral to the office. Both the student and the class are bewildered by the sudden, angry outburst. The permissive teacher's expectations and boundaries have become moving targets. In the end, the permissive teacher has a relationship, but little structure.

Permissive Elementary Scenario

Teacher:	Shawna, sit down.
	Shawna, you need to sit and focus on the task I have given you.
	Shawna, come and sit down and get working please.
	Shawna, what are you supposed to be doing right now?
	Shawna, give Dante back his pencil.
	Shawna, why are you out of your seat again?
	Shawna, move to the back and do your work there.
	Shawna, you don't need to throw that away right now. Go back to the seat I assigned you.
	Shawna, leave Amanda alone. You should not be

out of your seat right now.

Shawna, put that away; that's not what we are working on right now.

Shawna, that's it! Go to the office!

Permissive High School Scenario

Teacher:	Kevin, put the phone away.
Kevin:	I'm just charging it.
Teacher:	No, you're playing a game. Put it away.
Kevin:	Okay, in a second.
Teacher:	Now please.
Kevin:	Okay. *(Does not put it away.)*
Teacher:	*(After ignoring Kevin for a few minutes)* Okay that's enough. I told you to put that away 10 minutes ago.
Kevin:	Uh-huh. I'm almost done.
Teacher:	You need to be done right now.
Kevin:	Okay. Just a second.
Teacher:	*(Frustrated and frazzled)* Give me the phone.
Kevin:	I'm putting it away! Geez! Calm Down. *(Turns towards his backpack but continues using phone.)*
Teacher:	*(Seething)* Put the phone away or I'm taking it.
Kevin:	*(with condescending tone)* Okay, okay, I'm putting it away. *(Doesn't put it away.)*
Teacher:	*(Angry)* Kevin! Phone away now!
Kevin:	Okay! *(Slowly and dramatically puts phone away).* There. Done. All right? Better now? My phone is away.

Permissive teachers allow students too many chances to comply with their requests. They use no consequences at all when students evade, refuse, or choose not to comply. Instead, they simply continue making requests, which their students continue to ignore. Behaviorally, permissive teachers are teaching their students that it's optional to comply, when their intention is to be kind. The resulting dashed hopes, helplessness, and feelings of rejection they feel are what fuel their "snap." Maybe they throw the student out, as with Shawna, or simply escalate the tension in the room until eventually the student gives in, as with Kevin. Either way, students lose respect for these teachers and chronically ignore their requests.

The Authoritarian Teacher

Authoritarian teachers believe that the heavy hand is what's needed in education. If the local or national news carries a story about student misbehavior, you can bet the authoritarian teacher is having conversations with friends and colleagues about the need for teachers to be more strict and rigid. "If only the hammer had been dropped sooner, harder, and more often, then these things would have never happened," laments the authoritarian teacher. These teachers tolerate little, and frequently let everyone know it. Year after year, they also fail to connect with their most challenging students—and fail to support these students' academic learning.

The authoritarian teachers' strength is that they have clear boundaries. However, because of these boundaries, they are unwilling to take responsibility for any failures they have with difficult students. Instead, they blame the kids, the families, the administration, or society. They expect someone else to "fix" the kids, and only upon this "fixing" will they then try again to work productively with the students. These are the teachers who can sometimes be heard saying things like, "They have to meet me halfway," or "I can't be working harder than they are," or "You can lead a horse to water, but you can't make it drink."

A Closer Look

The authoritarian teacher seeks to change the student by force of will rather than through changes in conversation, connection, consequences, or tone.

The authoritarian teacher seeks to change the student by force of will rather than through changes in conversation, connection, consequences, or tone. Therefore, Tier 3 students rarely find success with authoritarian teachers, and often are seen seeking out other adults on campus to talk to. Many are searching for a sympathetic ear to plead their cases to. In the end, authoritarian teachers have structure, but no relationship.

Authoritarian Elementary Scenario

Shawna, why aren't you sitting?

You can sharpen your pencil later. Sit down.

I will not tolerate arguing! You sit down now!

That is arguing! Go to the office!

Authoritarian High School Scenario:

Teacher:	Kevin, give me the phone.
Kevin:	I'm just charging it
Teacher:	I said give it to me. Now.
Kevin:	Hold on. I'll put it away. I just need a second to finish this.
Teacher:	That's it. Go to the office!

In these examples, the authoritarian teacher escalates mild situations into office referrals, because they perceive student noncooperation and student attempts to defend themselves as personal attacks and challenges to their authority. Instead of being on the students' side — by modeling appropriate behavior, and helping them to learn to make good choices — these teachers lash out, to show the students who's boss. Behaviorally, authoritarian teachers are teaching their students that they — the teachers — don't have control over their own emotions, they don't care about their students, or they don't know how to use their position of authority to support their students. The result is that students lose respect for these teachers, and are more likely to resist them in the future.

Straight Talk

The authoritarian teacher escalates mild situations into office referrals.

Teachers & What *Does* Work

The middle ground, and what we spend our entire careers trying to find, is the balance between firm and soft. This is the place where empathy and structure meet. We call this the "chewy center." It is simultaneously firm and flexible, and it is the mainstay of an effective, balanced teacher.

The extremes of classroom management do not lead to long-term success. Effective teachers find success through a balanced approach. They have consistent structures and routines, they have clear boundaries, and they have care and connection. They float along the spectrum to meet the needs of unique situations and individual students. The difficult student is cared for, but not coddled and not spared consequences. The difficult student is also given the opportunity to fail — in order to learn valuable behavioral lessons — but isn't dismissed, devalued, or written off. Let's look at how a balanced teacher might have handled the cell phone issue with Kevin.

A Closer Look

Effective teachers live in the place where empathy and structure meet.

High School Scenario Revisited

Teacher:	Kevin, put the phone away.
Kevin:	I'm just charging it.
Teacher:	No, you're playing a game. Put it away.
Kevin:	Okay, in a second.
Teacher:	Kevin, you can put the phone away, or you can give it to me to hold until the end of the period. You have 10 seconds to choose. If the phone is not completely put away in 10 seconds, I will take the phone. *(Teacher turns or walks away and waits 10 seconds. Phone is not put away. Teacher returns.)*
Teacher:	Give me the phone.
Kevin:	I'm putting it away. Just hold on. I'm almost finished.
Teacher:	Kevin, you can give me the phone, and I will give it back to you at the end of the period,

> or you can go to the office and have them take it away and give it back at the end of the day. That's a much bigger deal and not what I want to have happen, but it's up to you. You have 10 seconds to place the phone on my desk. Not in your pocket, not in your backpack; on my desk. If it's not on my desk in 10 seconds, then you are choosing a referral to the office. *(Kevin puts the phone in his backpack.)*

Teacher: Head up to the office. I will send the referral up after you.

The balanced teacher above has found the chewy center. Their unspoken intention matches their words in being simultaneously firm and caring. First, they make a request. Next, when he doesn't originally cooperate, they offer Kevin a second chance to cooperate on his own. Third, they slowly and calmly increase the pressure and discomfort, in search of the place where Kevin can learn that they are serious. In this chewy center, the teacher can clearly communicate that they expect their reasonable requests to be complied with, while still demonstrating that they care about the student and his experience. Later in this chapter we will unpack exactly what balanced teachers are doing, how to do it, and why it works.

Straight Talk

The extremes of classroom management do not lead to long-term success. Effective teachers find success through a balanced approach.

PART 2: THE TOOLS

As the years progress, every teacher fills their "discipline toolbox" with strategies they learn from others, from professional development, and—most frequently—from trial by fire. We've found that some tools are definitely more effective than others with Tier 3 kids, but a list of consequences is simply not enough. The most effective approaches combine the flexible use of consequences and incentives, applied in creative ways, to foster specific positive behavioral outcomes.

Consequences — For Better or For Worse

Permissive teachers rarely use consequences, which causes them to jump to using too-large a consequence once they get exasperated. Authoritarian teachers use consequences vindictively to punish their students. Neither of these ways of relating to consequences is productive or ultimately effective.

Consequences in schools are meant to be used to teach behavioral lessons. When used effectively, they are not punishments. They are also not inherently bad or good, but simply the result of a student's choices or actions. Positive consequences reinforce actions and promote repetition. Negative consequences deter actions and promote change. This is the basis for all behavioral learning.

Food for Thought

Consequences are not inherently bad or good.

> *"Breaking a habit means that you break the link between the behavior and the reward it provides to you."*

— SUSAN KRAUSS WHITBOURNE,
PROFESSOR OF PSYCHOLOGY

For example:

▲ *Action:* You eat four donuts and have three cups of coffee for breakfast. *Consequence:* You feel tired and anxious all day.

▲ *Action:* You eat an egg-white omelet with spinach and turkey bacon and have a cup of green tea for breakfast. *Consequence:* You feel good and ready for your day.

▲ *Action:* You head to work driving 30 miles per hour over the speed limit because you're running late. *Consequence:* You get a speeding ticket.

▲ *Action:* You do an excellent job on a major project for your boss. *Consequence:* You receive recognition from your boss and coworkers.

In school we use consequences to teach behavioral lessons to reinforce desirable behaviors and deter undesirable behaviors.

▲ *Behavior:* A student writes an excellent paper.
   Consequence: The student earns an A, feels proud, and will likely work hard on the next paper.

▲ *Behavior:* A student writes an unreadable paper.
   Consequence: The student receives an F, feels sad or upset or embarrassed, and tries to do better on the next paper.

This is true until it isn't. As children get older, they might already have interacted for years in unsafe or unstable home or school environments, or have experienced severe trauma. They might have developed coping or defense mechanisms to protect themselves against the chronic, toxic stress they live in; these protective mechanisms can override or supersede traditional, behavioral learning paths. Unfortunately, these mechanisms are almost never in the students' long-term best interest. When protective mechanisms have "taken over," that's when we start to see both positive and negative consequences lose their impact. The A on the paper doesn't reinforce positive behavior, or the confiscated phone doesn't create enough, or the right kind of, discomfort to lead the student to make different choices in the future (For more on trauma and toxic stress, and how they affect brain development and behavior, see Appendix E).

A Closer Look

In school we use consequences to teach behavioral lessons.

When this happens, we move away from the traditional use of consequences—which are clearly not being effective and not leading to behavioral changes—and move toward formal and informal, one-on-one, specialized interventions. We will discuss these types of one-on-one interventions in chapter 5. But wait! Don't skip ahead to that chapter just yet. The over-identification of students who need unique, one-on-one, behavioral interventions is rampant in American schools. In truth, if we start by looking at improving our use of more traditional consequences and systems, then we can reduce the number and frequency of the behavioral problems we encounter. In this way, we can hone in more clearly on the students for whom traditional systems really won't work.

When a teacher is struggling with an entire class, or what they perceive to be a large number of students, almost always there are cracks in their classroom management dikes that need to be filled. Unfortunately, when the waters of misbehavior are leaking through from multiple places, and getting stronger and faster and more overwhelming, the drowning teacher can't see the individual cracks—or the possibility of filling them, little by little, over time. The teacher's distress at seeing the rising water level leads to tunnel vision and less-productive solutions, like screaming at the water to stop, or filling buckets with the water that's already come through and pouring it back into the lake on the other side of the dike. Sometimes it's necessary to take a step back to see the problem more clearly, and to plan more productive solutions. A first step is to assess where the leaks are coming from and then make a comprehensive plan to fill those cracks. One at a time.

Food for Thought

Sometimes it's necessary to take a step back to see the problem more clearly, and to plan more productive solutions.

Rigid Versus Flexible Consequence Hierarchies

Becoming a more effective disciplinarian isn't about finding some new, exotic consequence. It's about finding new ways to think about and use the consequences we already have to reinforce clear boundaries and teach behavioral lessons. In the process, it's also important to remember that "one size" does not fit all students.

Consequence hierarchies are meant to create a path you can follow when Tier 2 and Tier 3 students resist. In a traditional, step-by-step or lockstep hierarchy, the consequences on each successive step are supposed to be a little bit more uncomfortable than the consequences below them. In theory, as you progress up the steps, a student will eventually become uncomfortable enough to choose to cooperate with you, rather than choosing to suffer a very uncomfortable consequence. But all humans are different, and not everyone is made equally uncomfortable by the same things. For example, imagine that you have two children of your own. Your younger child hates being alone. Your older child prefers it. If you tell your younger child not to do something again or they'll be sent to their room, they'll think twice about doing it again—because the thought of being isolated in their room makes them very uncomfortable. But if you tell your older child to stop doing something or they'll be sent to their room, they're not at all deterred, because they love daydreaming alone in their room.

It's important to have a general path you can follow when students resist you. It's also important that the path be flexible enough to allow for detours and alternate routes, so that the path can be individualized to a particular student's needs. For example, when you move closer to James, who is off-task, he becomes a little uncomfortable and gets on task. You are happy with the result and now believe that "proximity," or moving closer to an off-task student, is an effective, mild consequence for redirecting student behavior. Later that hour, another student, William, is off-task. You move closer to him. But instead of getting uncomfortable and altering his

A Closer Look

Becoming a more effective disciplinarian isn't about finding some new, exotic consequence. It's about finding better ways to apply the consequences we already have.

Bright Idea

Create a flexible, leveled hierarchy of consequences.

behavior, he starts chatting with you and tries to draw you into his current distraction. Is proximity no longer an effective consequence? Of course not. But it's not effective for William. If you are locked into a lockstep hierarchy, like the one outlined below, and your mild redirect doesn't work, then theoretically, you'd now need to move up to something a little less mild or a little more confrontational. But that isn't fair to William. So what else can you do?

Rigid, Step-by-Step Hierarchy

Step 1:	▲ Verbal Warning
Step 2:	▲ Temporary Seat Change
Step 3:	▲ Loss of Something (time or points or privileges)
Step 4:	▲ Send to office

You can start by creating a flexible, leveled hierarchy of consequences, and move away from using rigid, step-by-step, or lockstep hierarchies. A one-size-fits-all discipline system, like the rigid hierarchy above, won't meet the needs of all students, and will likely only meet the needs of the least problematic students. You want to have a path you can follow if a student becomes apathetic, defiant, or confrontational, but you want flexibility in how you walk that path, as well.

A flexible, leveled hierarchy, like the one outlined on the next page, allows you to try two or three different mild things to redirect William before moving up the hierarchy. Ultimately this is better for both you and for William.

Flexible, Leveled Hierarchy

Level 1:   (Try 2 or 3 of these before moving to next level)

▲ Teacher looks at the student. (Teacher Look)

▲ Teacher says the name of the student.

▲ Teacher walks near the student. (Proximity)

▲ Teacher points at work student should be doing.

▲ Teacher reminds student of appropriate behavior.

▲ Teacher asks student what they should be doing.

▲ Teacher tells student to get back on task.

▲ Teacher reminds class of appropriate behavior.

▲ Teacher praises others for following directions / being appropriate.

▲ Teacher picks up grade book or walks closer to participation chart.

Level 2:   (Try 1 or 2 of these before moving to next level)

▲ Temporary seat change.

▲ Brief time-out, outside or back of room.

▲ Private conversation with teacher.

▲ Teacher writes warning note and passes it to student.

▲ Loss of a few participation points.

Level 3:   (Try 1 or 2 of these before moving to next level)

▲ Removal of individual privilege.

▲ Removal of potential group reward.

▲ Sent to another teacher for time-out.

▲ Rehearsal of expected rule/procedure.

▲ Brief recess or lunch detention.

▲ Phone call home to parent.

▲ Permanent seat change.

▲ Student completes a behavior reflection sheet.

Level 4:   ▲ Referral to office / Class suspension.

▲ Referral to counselor.

▲ Placed on behavior contract.

▲ Parent-Student-Teacher conference arranged.

▲ School community-service assigned.

▲ Schoolwide privilege removed.

▲ Student writes reflection on appropriate behavior.

To Post, or Not to Post

Many administrators and teachers feel it's important that teachers post or otherwise share with students their standard consequences, to create clarity, transparency, and accountability. There is certainly no harm in doing this, but it's also not necessary. Students learn who we are and what they can expect from us based on how we interact with them over time. Things posted on our walls, or shared on paper, are just words. Students know that talking the talk is not the same as walking the walk. Posting a hierarchy can be helpful, though, in reminding us of all the options we have at our disposal when we want to redirect a student or class.

Bright Idea

Post your leveled hierarchy of consequences as a pie chart.

If you decide that you do want to post your leveled hierarchy of consequences, then consider posting it as a pie chart, with each consequence listed on a different slice of the pie. This allows for greater flexibility in how we apply them and reminds us that our consequences are not a lockstep path to the office. You might also consider adding a consequence to the pie chart labeled "other." If you come up with a clever, improvised, natural consequence that perfectly fits a situation, but it isn't already listed on your hierarchy, then that "other" will have you covered.

Perhaps the best thing to do when choosing to post or share a discipline plan with students, and even parents, is to share the process, rather than the actual consequences. For what this process looks like, see the section later in this chapter titled "The WHAT of Effective Discipline."

Using Incentives & Rewards

As with anything else in education, rewards and incentives can be used effectively or ineffectively, depending on how they're implemented. The use of incentives to spur appropriate behavior has been much criticized for creating "extrinsic" motivation when our goal is "intrinsic" motivation. The theory is that if you're always offering rewards and incentives for correct behavior, then students won't learn to do things from a place of internal motivation, and they'll always expect to receive something in return for doing the right thing. Although it is possible to create that kind of situation, it is also possible to use incentives to help bridge the gap, when no internal or intrinsic motivation exists.

From Grace

When I first started teaching, my students operated at a low level, and the school had low expectations for their behavior and progress. Initially, I couldn't get many of my students to do anything for me. They wouldn't bring materials to class, do homework, come to class on time, or read silently during independent reading. They'd passively resist. I don't mean just a few kids. I mean a significant percentage of kids in every one of my high school classes. So I set up a classwide incentive program, where each class could earn points for particular things, with rewards for earning certain numbers of points. Of course, I chose the things I couldn't get them to care about as the primary point-earners. For example, if everyone was in class on time, 2 points. If everyone had a pencil, 1 point. If everyone brought a silent-reading book, 1 point. If everyone read during silent-reading time, 2 points. If everyone had their homework, 2 points. If nobody was absent, 2 points. The prizes ranged from a 30-minute screen party to reducing the final exam by half (students would only have to answer the even-numbered questions on the final exam). All of a sudden, kids were standing at my door seconds before the bell rang, yelling to other kids, "You have 13 seconds! Let's go!" Kids were running to class. Kids were reading. Kids were doing homework. It worked!

Bright Idea

When no intrinsic motivation exists, sometimes extrinsic motivators, such as prizes and incentives, can temporarily bridge the gap.

But in a couple of classes, I had scapegoats. Just one kid, sometimes two, in one or two of my periods would not buy in. After a couple of weeks, everyone hated these kids, because it was their fault the class wasn't earning points. To fix this, I tried a technique called "zero to hero." I told my 5th-period class that the one kid who was undermining the system would be exempt. For example, if that kid was the only kid not in class on time, they could still get their no-tardy points. BUT, if that kid was there on time, they got double points. So any time that kid did what was asked, the class was doubly rewarded. When that kid didn't do what was asked, the class didn't suffer for it. In this way, I fed my class's need and kept them on my side, while simultaneously encouraging my least-motivated student to try, even a little.

HOWEVER, although this worked initially to create some motivation with my classes at this school, it was a lot to keep track of and manage. Negotiations were constantly coming up. In the second semester, I stopped using this technique. When the kids asked why, I said because we didn't need it anymore. I told them that they now knew what they needed to do to be successful in my class, and they had learned to do it. They saw who I was and how much I cared about them, and they had matured past the point of needing incentives to do what was right and good for them and their education. They grudgingly agreed. I needed the system to hook them in while I proved I was a teacher worth respecting and working hard for. But once I had proved that in the first semester—through my consistency with holding boundaries in a caring but firm way, and my efforts to build relationships with them—I didn't need it in the second semester. Now we were on the same side. Intrinsic motivation had been created.

From Scott

When you are trying to change the culture of a school, one classroom at a time, the individual rooms make such a difference. My best teachers found ways to use their own personal systems of positive feedback and reinforcement to increase wanted behaviors. One common technique I saw, for example, was the use of the marble jar. The class earned marbles for achieving different goals, both procedural and behavioral—such as transitioning quickly, improvement in time on task, or responding to directions the first time given. When the jar was full, they earned a party or some other incentive set by the teacher. But each time they earned an incentive, the next empty jar was a little bigger, making it a little harder to earn the next incentive. In this way, the teachers were creating buy-in from students in working toward socio-behavioral endeavors—and celebrating their successes along the way.

To be clear, there is such a thing as too much reward. If you are running a ticket system and handing out tickets to individuals to reinforce good behaviors, consider handing them out only for exceptional behavior. A high-performing student who is normally well behaved should not get a ticket for sitting properly or having their materials, because it isn't exceptional behavior for them. On the other hand, those same behaviors might be exceptional for a student who is constantly struggling to listen and pay attention. For the higher-performing student, exceptional behavior might come in the form of being exceptionally helpful or encouraging to another student, or writing five paragraphs when they were only asked to write three. What is exceptional will be different for each student, but it should be

Straight Talk

There is such a thing as too much reward.

equally difficult to acquire a ticket, regardless. In this way, it's easier to manage the system, because you are giving out fewer tickets per day. This also creates equal opportunity for all students to receive a ticket, while simultaneously encouraging exceptional behavior and personal growth for all students, not just our highest-performing or best-behaved students.

Some might argue that tickets should be given to well-behaved students to reward them for making and modeling good choices. We do not advocate for that position here, for two reasons. First, students who find it easy to listen, follow directions, and stay focused are already receiving positive feedback in the form of high grades, increased self-esteem, and praise from adults. We're constantly reinforcing good behavior, in subtle and overt ways, in our well-behaved and high-performing kids. External motivators, like stickers and tickets, are used when we're trying to encourage a behavior that's not coming easily, when intrinsic motivation for the behavior is lacking. If you give out stickers and tickets and other extrinsic motivators for appropriate behaviors that are already in place, then the system undermines the kids' intrinsic motivation. Consequently, they start to expect prizes or rewards for doing anything and everything correctly, and get upset when the teacher sometimes fails to notice. This not only becomes impossible to manage, but it also ends in upset and resentment. Second, if you give out rewards for behaviors that are easy for some kids and hard for others, then you end up giving rewards most frequently to the kids who need the least encouragement. Those who most need the encouragement will rarely receive it. This is a case where equality is being championed over equity. In an equitable system, each student receives the support and encouragement they need, which will not be equal because their needs are not the same.

Straight Talk

If you give out extrinsic motivators for appropriate behaviors that are already in place, it undermines intrinsic motivation.

Do these types of incentive systems help when working with Tier 3 students? Sometimes. Generally, the few kids who don't buy into these incentive programs are Tier 3. So, although these systems don't necessarily meet the particular needs of all our Tier

3 students, they can help us to identify them and not over-identify Tier 2 students as Tier 3.

Is intrinsic motivation better than extrinsic motivation? Of course. Is offering rewards and incentives counter to this? Yes. But sometimes, when no internal motivation exists, a little external motivation is necessary to bridge the gap. That's okay. It's not forever. Phase it out over the year, or make it harder to earn the incentives as the year progresses. But if you are struggling with a truly unmotivated class or student, don't be afraid to try it out to see what it can do for you.

The Gentle Press

Nobody is better at finding the path of least resistance than kids. As it relates to classroom discipline, we have to make it more uncomfortable for our students to resist us than it is to cooperate with us. Otherwise, our students will simply continue to resist. If every interaction a resistant student has with us leads to an uncomfortable consequence, then eventually they will find it easier to cooperate. Over time, they will switch from general resistance to general compliance. This is especially true with students who resist passively. These students refuse to bring materials to class, refuse to work, or put their heads down regularly. Since it is easier to do nothing than it is to try, struggle, and possibly fail, they'll stick to that passive path of resistance as long as we allow it. If they are not disrupting the class, and we simply leave them alone — allowing them to do nothing — we silently communicate to them that we don't care if they learn. However, instead of allowing this pattern, we can show them our care by holding them in our hearts and using the "gentle press."

The "gentle press" is when we kindly but persistently apply pressure to a student to do more or better. If we gently but firmly confront them — by requiring them to talk to us, show us work, ask us questions, or talk with us outside — then we can sometimes

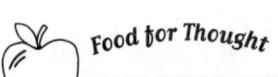
Food for Thought

We have to make it more uncomfortable for our students to resist us than it is to cooperate with us.

make them uncomfortable enough to try, just to get us off their backs. Then we both win.

Gentle Press Secondary Scenario

Teacher: *(To Chris, whose head is down.)* Chris, are you okay?

Chris: Yes. I'm just tired.

Teacher: Okay. That's fine. But you can't sleep in class. Can you sit up and work on the assignment, or do you need to step outside and get a drink of water first?

Chris: No. I'm fine. I'm just tired.

Teacher: Okay. Please sit up then.

    (Chris slumps up, does not pick up pencil.)

Teacher: Do you need help getting started?

Chris: No.

Teacher: Okay. Well, I need to see you writing on the assignment. I'm going to go check on some other students and then come back in a minute. If you are not writing on the assignment when I come back, I will help you some more.

    (Teacher circulates. Chris puts head back down. Teacher returns.)

Teacher: Chris, come outside with me for a minute. *(They go outside.)* Chris, how can I help you?

Chris: I don't need help. I'm just tired.

Teacher: Okay. But you can't have your head down in class. So here's what we can do. You take a couple of deep breaths out here and then come back in and start on the assignment. If you don't come back in, or if you come in but don't start writing on your paper, then I will know that you need to go to the office to talk to your counselor, see the nurse, or call home to have someone pick you up. Okay? Take

A Closer Look

The "gentle press" is when we kindly but persistently apply pressure to a student to do more.

a couple of breaths and then come on in. *(Teacher goes back inside. Chris enters, sits, picks up pencil, but closes eyes and does not work on assignment.)*

Teacher: Chris, here's a pass to the office. Please let your counselor or an administrator know that you aren't able to stay awake and need to see the nurse or call home.

In the secondary scenario above, any number of things might be going on with Chris. Maybe he really is just so tired that he cannot stay awake. Maybe some personal trauma is affecting his ability to focus and engage in class. Maybe he is under the influence of some illicit substance. Maybe the academic work is too hard for him, and he's evading it because trying makes him feel stupid. Regardless of the reason, the teacher needs to stay on his side, assume the best, and gently press him to start the assignment. In this way, the teacher expresses care both for him personally and for his academic success.

Gentle Press Elementary Scenario

Teacher: Chrissy, why aren't you working on the assignment?

Chrissy: I don't get it.

Teacher: What don't you get?

Chrissy: All of it.

Teacher: Okay, lets focus on the first question. What don't you get about question #1?

Chrissy: All of it.

Teacher: Hmm. Alright, let's go word by word. What does this word say?

Chrissy: "Dog."

Teacher: Excellent. Do you know what a dog is?

Chrissy: Yes.

Teacher: So that's not where you're stuck. Let's keep going. Read the first three words for me.

Chrissy: "The dog jumped...."

Teacher: Do you know what jumping is?

Chrissy:	Yes! I'm not stupid!
Teacher:	Okay. Hold on. I'm not trying to upset you. I am genuinely just trying to figure out where you are stuck. When I asked you what part of #1 you didn't understand, you said all of it. So now I'm trying to find out if it's really all of it, or just one part. Because then I can help you move forward. So let's keep going with #1.
Chrissy:	Okay, okay! I get #1.
Teacher:	Terrific, so you write your answer to #1, and then I'll come back and see how you are doing with #2.

In the elementary scenario above, Chrissy is resisting the learning. As with the secondary scenario, there are many potential causes for her resistance. By using the "gentle press," the teacher can stay on Chrissy's side and try to move her forward with the learning. If Chrissy gets triggered and explodes, then the teacher can take Chrissy outside to cool down, or send her to another location in the room. Then the teacher can try to find out what's behind Chrissy's resistance or upset, and choose a path forward from there.

PART 3: THE PROCESS

Effective behavioral intervention with Tier 3 students in a classroom happens when balanced teachers have the right tools and know how to best apply them. In other words, they don't just know what to do, they know how to do it. And, just as importantly, they know when to make exceptions and when to double-down.

The "What" of Effective Discipline

The "what" of effective discipline are the steps we take along the path to successfully end a disruption or teach a behavioral lesson. Generally speaking, the most common path to cooperation looks like this:

1: Reminder

2: Directive

3: Behavioral Choice

4: Consequence

5: Second Behavioral Choice

6: Second Consequence

7: Third Behavioral Choice

8: Third Consequence

For example, Jenny is being disruptive. Perhaps she's talking while others are talking, or jumping about in a way that's making it hard for the teacher to teach or for other students to learn.

1. Reminder:

"Jenny, this is a time for listening, not talking. Your turn to talk is coming." Or "Jenny, we're sitting still until I finish the directions."

Jenny continues to be disruptive.

2. Directive:

"Jenny, stop talking." Or "Jenny, sit down."

Jenny continues to be disruptive.

3. Behavioral Choice:

"Jenny, you have a choice. You can stop (name the disruptive behavior, such as talking while I am talking, getting up without permission, distracting others) or you can (name the consequence, such as move seats, take a time-out, change to a different task — whatever seems appropriate for that student in that moment). What would you like to do?"

Jenny says she will stop, but then continues to be disruptive.

4. Consequence:

"Jenny, move to the back with your work for a few minutes."

Or use some other consequence that seems appropriate, such as, "Jenny, step outside, take a breath, and come back in when you're ready to follow directions." After a few minutes, check in with her. Encourage her to try again and return to the group.

Jenny rejoins group or class but continues to be disruptive.

5. Second Choice:

"Jenny, you have a new choice. You can stop (name the disruptive behavior) or you can (name a more uncomfortable consequence this time, such as a permanent change of seat, completion of reflection sheet).

Jenny agrees to stop, but then continues to be disruptive.

6. Second Consequence:

"Jenny, move over here and complete this reflection sheet."

Jenny complies with the consequence, but then continues to be disruptive.

7. Third Choice:

"Jenny, you have a new choice. You can stop (name the disruptive behavior) or you can (name a very uncomfortable consequence this time, such as going to the office, or coming in at lunch or after school to complete work, or discussing behavior, or practicing following instructions.)

Jenny continues to be disruptive.

8. Third Consequence:

"Jenny, go to the office."

The "How" of Effective Discpline

Let's unpack the above interaction. Effectively intervening with resistant students and their misbehavior is not just about what we do. It's also about how we do it. This "how" includes the words,

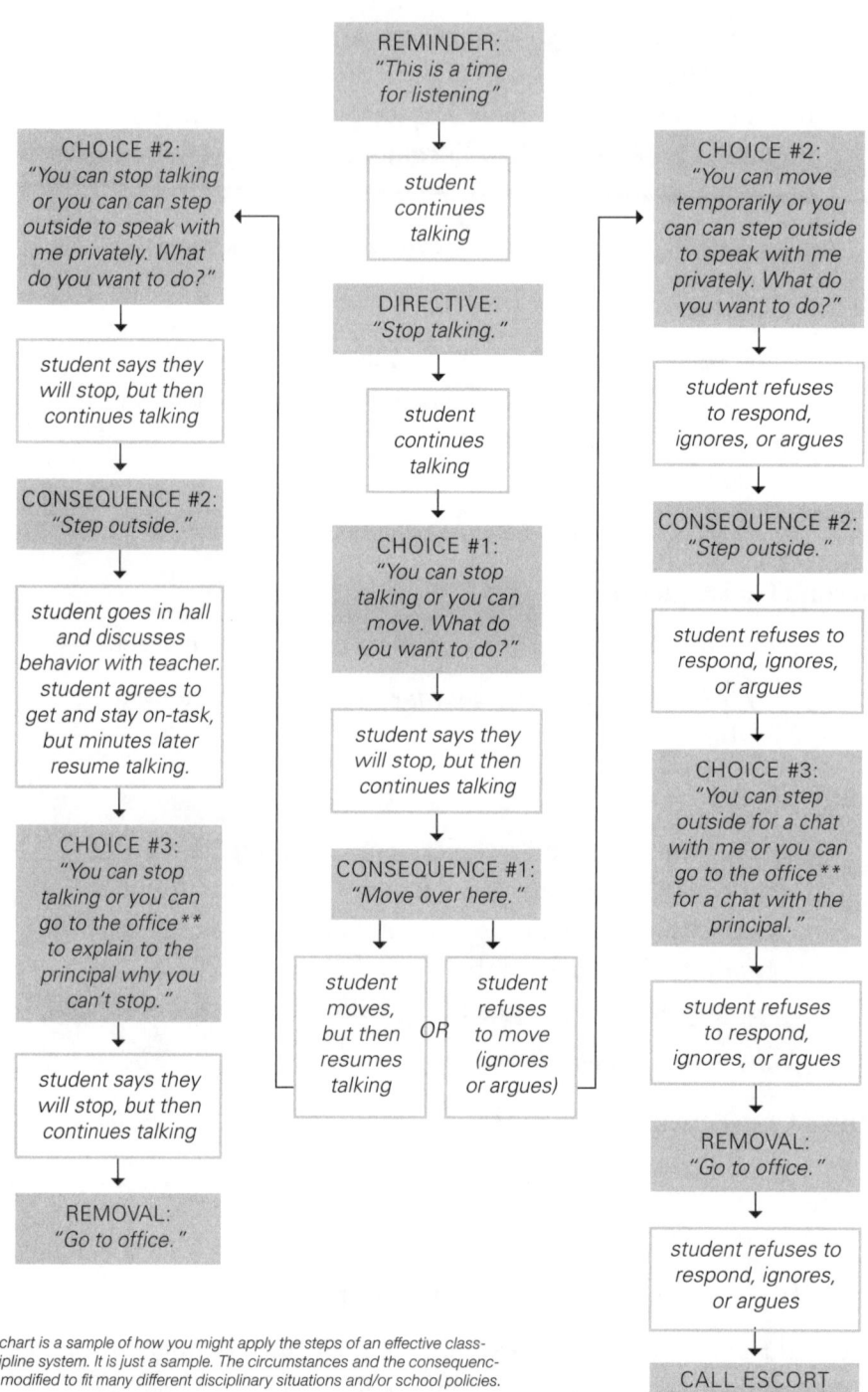

REMINDER:
"This is a time for listening"

student continues talking

DIRECTIVE:
"Stop talking."

student continues talking

CHOICE #1:
"You can stop talking or you can move. What do you want to do?"

student says they will stop, but then continues talking

CONSEQUENCE #1:
"Move over here."

student moves, but then resumes talking   *OR*   student refuses to move (ignores or argues)

CHOICE #2:
"You can stop talking or you can can step outside to speak with me privately. What do you want to do?"

student says they will stop, but then continues talking

CONSEQUENCE #2:
"Step outside."

student goes in hall and discusses behavior with teacher. student agrees to get and stay on-task, but minutes later resume talking.

CHOICE #3:
*"You can stop talking or you can go to the office** to explain to the principal why you can't stop."*

student says they will stop, but then continues talking

REMOVAL:
"Go to office."

CHOICE #2:
"You can move temporarily or you can can step outside to speak with me privately. What do you want to do?"

student refuses to respond, ignores, or argues

CONSEQUENCE #2:
"Step outside."

student refuses to respond, ignores, or argues

CHOICE #3:
*"You can step outside for a chat with me or you can go to the office** for a chat with the principal."*

student refuses to respond, ignores, or argues

REMOVAL:
"Go to office."

student refuses to respond, ignores, or argues

CALL ESCORT FOR HELP

*This flow chart is a sample of how you might apply the steps of an effective classroom discipline system. It is just a sample. The circumstances and the consequences can be modified to fit many different disciplinary situations and/or school policies.

**The office is not the only place that students might be removed to. You might, for example, send a student to a Buddy Teacher, a Trusted Adult, or a Counselor instead. See more about these options in Chapter 5.

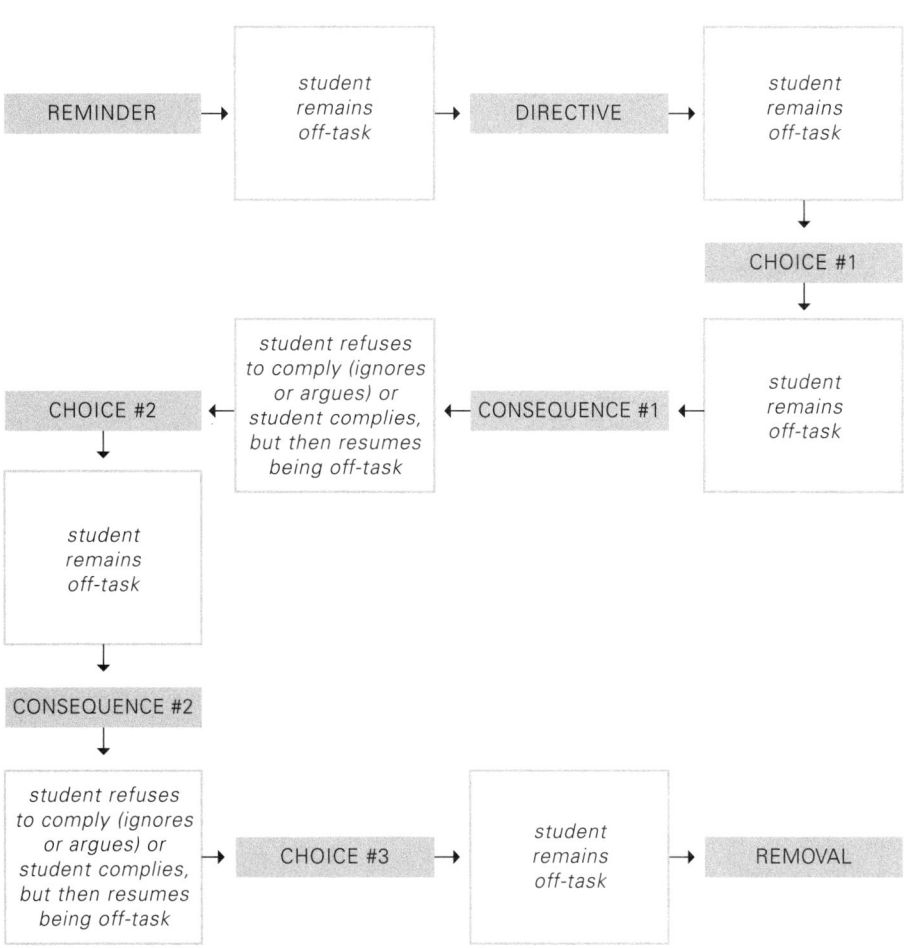

volume, and body language we use. In combination, these things communicate our unspoken intention to either support or punish. This is especially true when we need to de-escalate a tense situation.

The Words We Use — Offering Choices

The language of choice allows students to feel that they are in the seat of power. This is especially true of oppositional Tier 3 students. In order to feel safe and make good choices, they need to feel in control. Instead of saying to a student, "Danielle, stop it or I'll move you to the back," we say "Danielle, you have a choice. You can stop talking to your group about off-topic things, or you can move to the back to work on your own for a bit. What would you like to do?" Now she has the power to decide and is more likely to make a productive choice. She has no need to oppose the teacher, because the teacher is not telling her what to do; the teacher is just making clear to her what her choices are. She gets to decide how the interaction ends, based on which choice she makes.

Remember that it doesn't matter which choice Danielle makes. It doesn't matter because the purpose of the process is not to teach her to obey you, but is rather to teach her that her choices matter and that all her choices have consequences. This is harder to remember when Danielle continues to resist and becomes confrontational, and the choices become more uncomfortable. For example, Danielle chooses to stay with her group, but continues to disrupt. The teacher tells her to move to the back, because by continuing to disrupt, moving is actually the choice she has now made. But she refuses to go. Now what? For the answer to this question and more on how to de-escalate situations like this, see the section "Opposition & Escalation" later in this chapter.

The Voice We Use — Whisper Discipline

When offering students choices, the language we choose isn't enough on its own to create the safe and inviting feel that de-escalation requires. If we are angry or frustrated or feeling some other strong emotion during the interaction, we can use the language of choice while still communicating nonverbally that we are a threat. In addition to the language of choice, we need to use a quiet voice and a calm but firm demeanor.

In behavioral situations, yelling doesn't communicate confidence or strength. It communicates weakness. It communicates to students that we've lost control and are now a loose cannon. Anything can happen. The environment is now toxic and unsafe. One way to combat the urge to yell is to practice "whisper discipline." Whisper discipline is the practice of lowering your voice to as close to a whisper as possible. Try this whenever you switch from teaching content to teaching behavior. The lowered volume creates a shift in the environment without creating an environment that feels dangerous. It also helps to reduce the embarrassment factor for the student being disciplined. On its own, though, whisper discipline isn't enough. We can all think of a time when we saw someone whispering to try to control their anger, but it still came out as threatening, through clenched teeth and angry eyes.

Straight Talk

In behavioral situations, yelling communicates weakness.

The Body Language We Use — Soft Eyes

The final piece necessary to ensure that you are not the one escalating a disciplinary situation is to combine your lowered voice and offering of choices with "soft eyes."

From Grace

When I was a new teacher, I found myself in confrontations with kids all the time. I started teaching when I was 23 at a low-performing, high-poverty, urban high school. I was young, immature, inexperienced, and working in a tough school with at-risk teens. Because of this combination, I sometimes could not keep the frustration out of my voice and body language when students resisted, argued, or confronted me. As a result, I unintentionally escalated many interactions. In my third year, I got a new mentor teacher who, after observing me one time, asked me to try using a technique called "soft eyes." She said if I concentrated on keeping the muscles around and between my eyes completely soft, or neutral, when students confronted me, then my voice and body language would automatically soften. I could then convey calm and control to the student, rather than fear or frustration. She told me that it's a physiological impossibility to have an edge in your voice or be threatening in your body language if the muscles around and between your eyes are soft. You know what? It's 100% true! Try it in the mirror or with a friend.

To be safe, respectful, compassionate, and a good role model for our students during tense interactions, we need to be calm. We need that calm to be expressed both verbally and nonverbally. This kind of calm is often a natural byproduct of assuming the best about our students and seeing their misbehavior as a request for help. But even if we haven't quite internalized these positive assumptions yet, we can make progress toward them when we use the language of choice, soften our eyes, and lower our volume to de-escalate volatile situations. The use of these techniques creates an environment in which the student has the highest probability of making a productive choice. They still might not make the choice we want, and that's okay. Sometimes in order to learn, students must test all the way to the wall to see what lies on the other side. That's part of the process. However, when we are calm and clear, at least we know that we weren't the reason why they went all the way to the wall. We know that we did everything we could to help them learn an appropriate behavioral lesson. We strengthened our student-teacher relationship, rather than weakening it.

Opposition & Escalation

It is not uncommon for Tier 3 students to seem oppositional, and they might even have been diagnosed with Oppositional Defiance Disorder (ODD). Regardless of a diagnosis, however, students demonstrating oppositional behaviors tend to react very poorly to being told what to do. They might get angry, argue, confront, or lash out, even when they know this is an overreaction. This is in part because oppositional students often perceive directives from authority figures as personal threats or attacks, triggering the fight-or-flight response in their brains. (See Appendix E for more on how and why this happens). When a student like this gets triggered and confronts or defies, things can get heated and out of hand very quickly. If we keep our heads, look for the invisible subtitle, and use soft eyes, quiet voices, and the language of choice, then we can diffuse the situation — or at least stay on the student's side and teach them an appropriate behavioral lesson. For example, imagine that a teacher has asked a student named David to change seats, but David has refused. The next step might sound like this:

Bright Idea

Lower your voice to as close to a whisper as possible whenever you switch from teaching content to teaching behavior.

Teacher:	"David, you have a choice. You can move temporarily to the back on your own, where I can help you and we can work this out. Or, you can choose to step outside with me and have a private conversation about why you won't move to the back. It's up to you. I'll give you 20 seconds to decide. If you're not in the seat I asked you to move to in 20 seconds, we will go outside together."

After making David's choices clear, the teacher walks away and helps another student or goes on with instruction for half a minute. *Walking away when a student needs to make a tough decision is essential.* If you stay, it increases the threat level the student feels, and they're less likely to make a productive choice. In a nutshell, the process we follow with oppositional students who refuse to comply with reasonable requests is: **Choice, Timeline, Walk Away.** David is offered a behavioral choice, given a timeline in which to make his decision, and left alone to make it on his own. But let's imagine that the 20 seconds have gone by and David has chosen not to move.

David:	*(Ignores teacher's request and doesn't move.)*
Teacher:	David, come outside with me for a moment. It's okay. You aren't in trouble. We just need to speak privately for a second.
David:	*(Refuses, passively or aggressively, to step outside.)*
Teacher:	David, you have a new choice. You can come outside with me so we can work this out, which is what I want and what I hope you choose, or you can choose to go to the office and talk this out with the principal, instead. It's up to you. I will give you half a minute to decide. If you're not outside by then, then I'll write the referral. *(Teacher walks away and helps another student or goes on with instruction for half a minute.)*
David:	*(Ignores teacher and remains at his desk or gets up and roams around.)*
Teacher:	David, here's your referral. Go to the office, please.
David:	*(Refuses, passively or aggressively, to go to the office.)*
Teacher:	David, you can choose to go on your own to the office or you can choose to have me call for an escort to take you there. I'm going to walk away now, but if you're not heading to the office in the next minute, then I'll call for someone to come get you. *(Teacher walks away.)*

| David: | (Refuses to respond, or argues, or explodes.) |
| Teacher: | (Calls for support and has David removed.) |

No matter how David chooses in any of the above interactions, and even if he ends up in the office, he learns the right behavioral lesson. He learns that the teacher is serious when they make a request, but they will not embarrass him or lash out at him. He learns that noncooperation ends in immediate discomfort, though this discomfort will come gently and from a place of care. He learns that the teacher will always give him a choice before they give a consequence, because they're on his side, even when they're disciplining him.

Doubling-Down on Consequences

With resistant students, it is often necessary to temporarily isolate them in order to have a private or quiet conversation about their behavioral choices. This private interaction is much more productive when it does not occur front and center, for the class to witness. The most common ways to do this are to temporarily move a student to the back of the room or into the hallway. When you get to this point in a disciplinary interaction, the student will sometimes up the ante by cooperating on the surface (i.e., moving) but be disruptive while doing it. This is a tricky scenario. On one hand, they are complying with your request, but on the other hand, they are creating a new behavioral infraction in the process. If you double-down on the consequences, by adding a second consequence for the disruption, then you risk escalating the interaction. However, if you ignore the second disruption, then you risk sending the message that the behavior is permissible—which in turn encourages the student to continue doing it in future interactions.

A Closer Look

Sometimes in order to learn, students must test all the way to the wall to see what lies on the other side.

A Closer Look

Oppositional students often perceive directives from authority figures as personal threats or attacks, triggering thier freeze-fight-or-flight response.

In Chapter 2 we talked about how student misbehavior is a test. This is a common version of such testing. The student's invisible subtitle here might be, "I'm angry and embarrassed that my choices have landed me in trouble, and I don't know how to express these feelings appropriately. Please help me." In the following two stories from Grace and Scott you will see two common versions of how this occurs in classrooms and how they might be handled. Our goal is to take a balanced approach and to live in the chewy center of discipline.

From Grace

Jessica was an 11th-grader who was not doing her work and was being distracting to others. The teacher I was observing attempted to redirect Jessica's focus in several different ways. Eventually, the teacher decided that a private conversation was necessary, and told Jessica to go out into the hall. Jessica walked toward the door, but as she went she said very loudly, in a voice dripping with sarcasm, "Ohhhh, no. I guess I'm in big trouble now. I have to go 'outside' for a talking-to." The teacher followed Jessica into the hallway and simply said, "Keep going" and pointed toward the office. The rest of their interaction then went like this:

Jessica: What? What did I do?

Teacher: You did this: "Oh no, I'm in trouble..."
(Mimics Jessica's sarcasm.)

Jessica: *(feigning incredulity)* So?! I went into the hall like you asked. You never said I had to go without talking. You can't send me to the office for that.

Teacher: You and I both know that was disrespectful

> and disruptive. That's not acceptable in my class. Go to the office.
>
> **Jessica:**   What the F-ck!
>
> **Teacher:**   *(Silently points to the office.)*
>
> **Jessica:**   Come on!
>
> **Teacher:**   *(Silently points to the office.)*
>
> **Jessica:**   F-cking A--hole! *(Storms off to the office.)*

In the above story, Jessica was sent outside as a consequence for her off-task behavior, but on the way there she escalated the situation by being disrespectful and disruptive to the entire class. This disruption was a second, separate infraction from the one that got her sent out of the room. As such, it deserved a second, separate consequence.

One could argue that Jessica was right. The teacher did not explicitly say she could not talk as she went to the hall. However, it's unreasonable to think that a teacher must explicitly describe every way in which a student should not misbehave. The absence of a laundry list of "don'ts" does not mean that students have carte blanche to be disruptive or disrespectful whenever they are asked to do something they don't want to do. If the teacher lets Jessica's disruption pass, then Jessica learns that she is allowed to be disruptive and disrespectful whenever she is given a consequence—and she will consequently continue to be so in future disciplinary interactions. This will continue until she receives an uncomfortable consequence for this behavior. One could also argue that the teacher should have given Jessica one more chance, saying

Bright Idea

Walking away when a student needs to make a tough decision is essential.

Bright Idea

With resistant students, it is often necessary to temporarily isolate them in order to have a private or quiet conversation.

something along the lines of, "I will let it go this time because it's the first time—but next time I ask you to do something and you respond like that, you will be sent to the office. Understood?" Yes, the teacher could do that, the first time. But only the first time. Nine times out of ten, when students are given second chances of this kind, they repeat the same behavior within 24 hours. That doesn't mean we shouldn't give them the benefit of the doubt or the second chance. It just means we shouldn't be surprised or upset when they repeat the behavior almost immediately, because this is a test. And we haven't passed it yet. Until we pass the test, by holding them gently but firmly accountable for the disrespectful behavior, they don't believe we really care if they do it or not.

From Scott

I was observing a 4th grade class when an off-task student was told to move temporarily to the back of the room. He went, but he made a big scene about it. He banged on his desk as he got up, he muttered something about hating the teacher, he knocked another student's materials off their desk as he walked by, and he kicked the desk at the back of the room a couple of times before eventually yelling "this is stupid!" and dramatically slumping into it with his head down over crossed arms. The teacher ignored the student's outburst temporarily and went on with her lesson as best she could. After a few minutes, the teacher gave the rest of the class a task to work on and went to the back to talk with the student. He wouldn't look at her or pick up his head, so she wrote him a quick note that basically expressed her concern for him and asked him to write her a reply telling her how he was feeling and also asking him to brainstorm two possible ways he might make amends to his classmate whose materials he threw to the ground. Then she returned to the front of the class and continued with her lesson. When the class transitioned into literacy rotations a little later, she pulled the student aside and they talked it out. He ended up apologizing to the student he had wronged and he also gave that student one of his treasure box coupons. And he had to spend some of his free choice time that afternoon practicing with the teacher how to move to the back of the room appropriately when asked.

As with Jessica, the 4th grade student in Scott's story above deserved and received two separate consequences. The first consequence was being temporarily sent to the back of the room for being off-task. The second consequence, attached to the way he went there, was to apologize, give up a treasure coupon, and practice during his free-choice time a different way of responding to the teacher's requests. As a result of these additional consequences, the student learned that even if he is upset, there is a line of appropriateness — and he must learn to respect it.

As with all of life's lessons, there are exceptions to the "doubling-down" rule. Let's say I tell a student to go to the hall, or to the back of the room, and the student is upset. They quietly mutter "F-ck" to themselves as they go. Do I double-down on the consequences, because they had feelings they could not suppress while changing locations? No, I don't. But if they say "f-ing a--hole," loudly enough for me and others to hear, then yes, I do. Every situation is different. The chewy center of teaching behavioral

Straight Talk

Nine times out of ten, when students are given second chances they repeat the same behavior within 24 hours.

lessons is finding the balance between being flexible and firm. Permissive teachers err toward being flexible to the point that no real discomfort is applied and no lesson is learned. Authoritarian teachers err toward being firm such that the lesson is learned but resentment is also created, which fuels the student's desire for revenge. The balanced teacher is able to find the chewy center, making judgment calls based on individual circumstances about how flexible to be at what times.

Sometimes Kids Must Be Sent Out

There is a pervasive myth in education that sending students out of class equals a loss of the teacher's power. The thought is that somehow the student wins if they are sent out to someone else for intervention or discipline. This isn't true. When used correctly, sending a student to someone else for discipline communicates a clear boundary. There is a line, and once someone has crossed it, they can no longer continue to be a part of your class, at least temporarily.

Analogies from parenting have been used to support this myth. Imagine a scenario where your child is misbehaving. You try several things, but they won't stop, so you send them to your spouse for further discipline. Now the child knows you can't handle the situation yourself, and that you "need" your spouse to step in and lower the boom. The child now perceives you as weak and your spouse as strong.

Although this analogy is seductive, it is false. Teaching in a school is not parenting in a home. A teacher's attempt to discipline a disruptive student while 30 others are waiting to learn is not the same as a parent's disciplining a disruptive child at home. This is true regardless of the number of siblings in the family. At the moment of discipline, your other children do not necessarily need your attention while you focus on a disruptive child.

A more apt analogy from parenting is when your child refuses to cooperate with a reasonable request, and you make several attempts

A Closer Look

A balanced teacher is able to make judgment calls about how and when to be flexible.

to get them to comply. Ultimately, they cross the line and receive a large and uncomfortable consequence, such as being grounded or having their screen time reduced or having their cell phone taken away. That's not how you wanted it to end, and you tried to have a more productive outcome without having to take their phone, screens, time, or freedom. But due to their continued poor choices, it became in their best interest to receive a large consequence. The application of this consequence allows them to learn that there is a line, and on the other side of that line is discomfort.

In school, the large and uncomfortable consequence on the other side of the line happens outside your room with another adult. But it is not a loss of power. It's a reinforcement of power. Loss of power happens when you don't send the student out, and they're allowed to continue defying or disrupting. When this happens, you teach the behavioral lesson that there is only so much you can do—and if they resist all of it, and can live with the discomfort of your in-class consequences, then they can continue the misbehavior indefinitely.

Please remember, however, that what happens after you send a student out is controlled by someone else. So, although it is not a loss of power to send a student out, it is a loss of control. Setting boundaries is essential. You control where the boundary is, and you communicate that to the student and the class. But someone else controls the student's ultimate consequence or intervention once they leave your room. Conflict and resentments arise when the teacher does not agree with or does not understand the consequences or intervention given by another authority figure. This can be resolved or avoided by clear communication among all affected parties about what office discipline and schoolwide interventions are and aren't, how common scenarios will generally be handled, and when and why there will be exceptions. See more on schoolwide discipline in Chapters 5 and 6.

A Closer Look

It is not a loss of power to send a student out. But it is a loss of control.

Finally, it is possible to lose power when sending a student out. Some teachers overuse the consequence of sending students to the office or to other adults, referring students too often for too many infractions and for infractions that could have been handled in the classroom. The difference between losing power and reinforcing power while sending a student out depends largely on why, when, and how you do it.

For example, if you are frustrated and out of patience with a kid, and send them out because you just can't deal with them any longer, then you are giving up power. But if you have made multiple, calm, reasonable, progressive attempts to get and keep the student on task, and the student continually chooses to disrupt anyway, then sending them out is not a loss of power. It's just the next reasonable consequence to give. When all your attempts come to naught, and the student needs a kind of support that you cannot provide with 30 other kids in the room, then sending them out is sometimes what should happen.

Bright Idea

Pick just one new thing to try. Try it for two weeks.

Unfortunately, some teachers send kids out before they have made multiple reasonable, progressive attempts, including nonverbal attempts, to appropriately redirect the behavior. This might happen because the teacher doesn't know what to do — perhaps they lack either experience or knowledge of alternative strategies — or because they are frustrated, have lost patience, and are now unconsciously wanting to punish rather than support. As with many moments in education, the subtleties of our unspoken intention play a big part in determining whether we are being effective or ineffective, proactive or reactive.

Take One Step Forward

This chapter includes many suggested changes for improving interactions with Tier 3 students. But making a lot of changes all at once can be overwhelming. Even the thought of it can lead to emotional paralysis. Our suggestion is to pick just one new thing to try. Try it for two weeks. If you do it incorrectly or it doesn't work, don't give up. Try again. Journal or reflect on any failures and missteps. Modify. Try again. Don't beat yourself up. Change is hard. Automaticity takes time to develop. Have faith. It will come. Or, get your colleagues involved. Get out of your own room and learn from the experts around you! The days of being the lone teacher working in isolation and separate from peers are long gone. Use the people around you to do peer observations, or videotape a lesson to watch later and examine your novel attempts and their outcomes. Teachers can learn so much from one another and from watching themselves via video.

Bright Idea

Have a trusted colleague observe you teach, or record yourself teaching and watch it back. The feedback will be invaluable.

Getting better at addressing off-task and defiant behaviors in the classroom takes time, patience, and practice. If you've never attempted to interact with kids by keeping your voice low, your eyes soft, and offering choices, then your first attempts will likely be uncomfortable, especially if you perceive this as not being "your style." But we aren't paid to have a style. We are paid to take kids from where they are and move them forward, academically and behaviorally. If your style isn't accomplishing that, then it's on you to change, even if it's uncomfortable. In addition, just because you know what to do does not mean you can do it right out of the gate. This kind of change requires practice, especially when we are working in real time, when emotions are high, feelings are triggered, or situations are volatile. How long does it take? Our experience shows that starting to get comfortable with a new technique, strategy, or way of doing things takes about three months. By then, you should feel that you are kinda, sorta getting it. Then, expect to take about three years to master it, just as with teaching content.

We accept that getting comfortable with teaching a new grade level or content area will take about three years. We understand that Year 1 is for experimenting, Year 2 is for modifying, and Year 3 is for flourishing. Yet, many of us don't give ourselves the same space to learn new ways of intervening with misbehavior. When we try a new behavioral technique or new

A Closer Look

To get comfortable with a new technique, strategy, or way of doing things takes about three months.

disciplinary system, we tend to give up after a few weeks if we don't see the outcome we expected, if it doesn't work seamlessly, or if it's a struggle to implement. Change happens slowly. You have to start with belief in the possibility and realistic expectations. Believe that you can eventually do it. Be realistic about how quickly it might, or might not, happen. Make peace with the fact that you will do it wrong many times before you do it right — and remember that doing it wrong isn't failure, it's just part of the process.

▲ ▲ ▲

Yeah Buts & What Ifs…

> **Teacher: What if offering choices doesn't work, and the student won't comply — and ends up in the office or sent out somewhere else?**

That's okay! Be at peace. Just because the student felt the necessity to test you all the way to the wall and never made a productive choice, or the choice you hoped for, that doesn't mean the system isn't working. Noncompliance is part of the learning curve. Students get to make their own choices. The system is about making their choices clear to them in advance, so they see that they are in control of, and responsible for, the outcome. That's where behavioral learning occurs. Some kids do not need to test at that level. Others do. Still others need to test all the way to the wall multiple times in order to learn a lesson or to trust that the adult will stay safe and treat them with respect, no matter what. Stay consistent and calm, and be on their side in your heart. It will pay off eventually.

Straight Talk

Make peace with the fact that you will do it wrong many times before you do it right.

Teacher: What if I offer a student a choice and they refuse to respond?

Refusal to choose is still a choice. The student chooses what you want, or, by default they have chosen the other way. When they are silent or refuse to respond, try telling them that you will give them a few seconds to decide and show you which choice they want to make. Then walk away. (This is the "Choice, Timeline, Walk-Away" technique). After 20 to 30 seconds, if they have still not complied with either choice, then go back, apply the consequence, and offer a different set of choices ("up" the discomfort).

A Closer Look

Student non-compliance is a normal part of the behavioral learning process.

Teacher: What about students who really don't care?

Our willingness to work productively with difficult kids cannot be predicated upon their caring. It's not our students' job to care. It is *our* job to care and to prove it in our every word and action.

This is easier said than done, though. When a student says they don't care about math or about succeeding academically, we still apply pressure to support them in trying and learning. We get creative in our attempts to inspire or motivate them. We search for ways to convince them of the importance of the learning. We develop new ways of presenting the content to make it more accessible, more palatable, more enticing, or more relevant. Few of us have been aware of the need to put this kind of energy, thought, and creativity into teaching appropriate behavior, however.

In the end, no matter how a kid might try to convince us that they don't care, they really do. We must remember, however, that sometimes some kids cannot express care. The worlds they live in just aren't safe enough for them to be that vulnerable. We need to understand that some kids not only can't express how much they care; they also actually can't feel it, because they have such a fortress of defenses up around them. It's easier to remember this and hold onto positive beliefs with kids who present as apathetic, withdrawn, or fragile. It's so much more difficult to do this with kids who present as belligerent, confrontational, manipulative, or just plain mean. It's our life's work as teachers to learn to see the best in the students who push our buttons the most, and to treat them with love and respect, even when we have to "fake it until we make it."

Teacher: What if I have multiple Tier 3 students in the same class or period?

Unfortunately, there is no magic strategy that will resolve this situation. But there are steps we can take to make productive headway.

1. Check in with the other adults who interact with these students and find out what works for them. You might contact parents, administrators, other teachers (general-ed and special-ed), counselors, or the school psychologist.

2. Look to anything you can alter in your learning environment that might contain or reduce their misbehaviors. For example, are there ways you can tighten up the reinforcement of your procedures and routines? Can you be more clear and consistent in the way you give directions? Can you introduce small modifications or differentiate lessons in a way that will better meet their academic skill levels?

3. Practice the ideas in this chapter regarding redirecting off-task behavior and intervening with misbehavior. Are you calmly, with soft eyes and whispered voice, giving them choices and following through with appropriate consequences when they misbehave? Are they feeling the discomfort that is the result of their inappropriate behavioral choices?

4. Start to strategically build stronger relationships with these students. Find out about their interests and background and

weave personal connections and conversations into your interactions with them.

5. Either start a one-on-one intervention plan with one student, as described in Chapter 5, or start a group intervention that focuses on an area of need common to all of your Tier 3 students. While the common issue might not be each student's area of highest need, it will still benefit all of them to work toward behavioral improvement in any area, and it will reduce your personal energy expenditure.

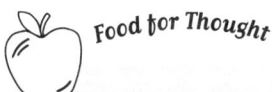

Food for Thought

It's our life's work as teachers to learn to see the best in the students who push our buttons the most.

Administrator: What if district policy is that teachers can't take cell phones away from students?

That's okay. The cell phone consequence described in the cell phone example was not meant to be a script for how all technology-related problems should be handled. It is just one way to do it, and the subject is relevant in today's classrooms. No matter your school's available interventions, our example explains the general concept of how a teacher might move up their hierarchy quickly but fairly, using the language of choice. If you can't allow teachers to take away student cell phones, then instead encourage them to choose something else that is within district policy. Perhaps the choice is to put the phone away or take a zero for the warm-up activity, or get a phone call home to parents, or come in at lunch to have a private conversation and complete the work you should have completed while you were messing around with your cell phone, or go to the office to discuss with an administrator why you are unwilling to follow directions and comply with classroom rules. The key is that your teachers must have some options that create discomfort for their students when their students refuse to put their cell phones away. If teachers don't have any uncomfortable consequences available, then the student has no motivation to cooperate, and the teacher's authority is undermined.

> **Administrator: What if our school policy is that teachers should not send students to the office on a referral unless the student is being a danger to self or others?**

In brief—change the policy. We discuss more detailed answers to this question in Chapters 4 and 6.

▲ ▲ ▲

Summary & Applications

Remember

- ▲ Kids act out and/or resist in order to feel in control or safe.

- ▲ Giving students too many chances to cooperate is just as ineffective as not giving them enough chances. Look for ways to stay in the "chewy center" of being firm but caring.

- ▲ Rigid, step-by-step-consequence hierarchies are usually ineffective with Tier 3 students. They don't meet the unique needs of these students whose behavioral learning paths might have been disrupted by toxic stress and childhood trauma. Flexible, leveled hierarchies allow for greater potential success.

- ▲ With shut-down and apathetic students, employ the "gentle press" to stay on their side as you apply pressure to help them to move forward.

- ▲ Oppositional students respond better to behavioral choices than to directives.

- ▲ The "how" of discipline is just as important as the "what." Kids respond to our Unspoken Intention, our body language, and our tone of voice, more than our words.

- ▲ Make peace with your own feelings of resistance around confronting kids when their behavior needs to change. Teaching behavior is messy and uncomfortable, but it cannot be avoided.

Discuss

- ▲ Do you recognize yourself in the description of either the permissive or authoritarian teachers? What is one step you might take, or change you might make, to move closer to being in the chewy center?

- ▲ Think of a Tier 3 student you've worked with in the past. What positive and negative consequences did you use to try to help them alter their behavior? Which were most effective? Why do you think this was so?

- ▲ Are there any consequences listed on the "Leveled Hierarchy" in this chapter that you might add to your repertoire, or your hierarchy, to give you more flexibility and to help you better meet individual student needs?

- ▲ Under what sets of circumstances have you sent a student out of your classroom to another adult for intervention or discipline? What steps did you take in these situations to first try to de-escalate the situation, and to keep them in the learning environment? In retrospect, are there any other things you could've tried?

- ▲ What incentives are you using with your class as a whole and/or with individual Tier 3 students to support their behavioral learning? What problems are you coming up against in using these? Brainstorm possible solutions to these problems.

Apply

- ▲ **Create** a leveled hierarchy with at least six consequences listed on the first level and at least four consequences listed on each successive level. **Role-play** with a friend or colleague how you might progress through the levels with a particular student who's currently driving you crazy, or drove you crazy last year. Consider having your hierarchy at your fingertips. Try carrying it around the room with you as a list on your cell phone, or on a laminated card, so you can refer to it as necessary, in real time.

▲ When students confront, defy, or resist, practice using the phrase, "You have a choice right now." Use soft eyes and speak in a quiet voice as you offer them a choice to get back on task or receive a reasonable consequence. Try it for two weeks. If you do it incorrectly or it doesn't work, don't give up. Try again. Journal, reflect, or discuss with a trusted colleague any failures and missteps. Modify. Try again.

▲ Role-play with a trusted friend or colleague a particularly bad moment you can remember having with a student. Practice handling it differently.

▲ At the end of each day, journal, or in some other way reflect upon, any difficult behavioral interactions you had that day. What did you handle well? What could you have handled better? What were the possible Invisible Subtitles that you missed? What was your Unspoken Intention when things escalated? How will you handle similar situations better in the future? Give yourself three months. Don't let initial failures or stumbling blocks stop you.

▲ Videotape yourself teaching and review the video—alone, or with a trusted colleague, friend, or family member. Look for the places where you tried new techniques and discuss how they worked out and how they could be improved upon. Look for blow-ups and bad moments, and discuss what you can do differently next time. Note: Generally, you don't need permission to videotape if you are not going to post, upload, or share it anywhere, but double-check this with your administration.

4

SCHOOLWIDE DISCIPLINE

> *"The power of one, if fearless and focused,
> is formidable, but the power of many
> working together is better."*
>
> — GLORIA MACAPAGAL ARROYO,
> SPEAKER OF THE HOUSE OF THE PHILIPPINES

S CHOOLWIDE DISCIPLINE AND INTERVENTION SYSTEMS, exist to support both those students who need only minimal, intermittent support in controlling their behavior and students who need constant and continual support. In this chapter, we explore concepts, techniques, and systems that can support you and your school in working more effectively with both groups—but in particular with the latter. We start by describing common problems and gaps that exist in schoolwide and office-based behavioral supports. We end with two sets of solutions: discipline-based ideas, such as the use of office consequences to teach behavioral lessons; and intervention-based ideas, such as the use of special environments, programs, and personnel to meet the emotional needs of Tier 3 students.

▲ ▲ ▲

Ineffective Office Discipline

No matter how effective a teacher is—at redirecting off-task behaviors, intervening with defiance, and de-escalating confrontations—sometimes a student is so disruptive, and so resistant to being redirected, that sending them out of the room is the most effective option. If done for the right reasons, this decision serves the best interests of the teacher, the class, and the student. But where do you send them? And what happens there? Being sent out of class should not be a reward or so pleasurable that the student returns feeling vindicated, but neither should it be so punitive that the student returns just as upset as when they left.

Ineffective schoolwide discipline comes in several different forms, and might look very different in different schools. It also can occur for a variety of different reasons.

Straight Talk

Sometimes a student is so disruptive, and so resistant to being redirected, that sending them out of the room is the most effective option.

From Grace

In one high school where I worked, an assistant principal routinely sent students back to class from the office after only the briefest of conversations and with no apparent change in the student's attitude. In one week, two of my colleagues reported that when students returned to class after office visits, they said, respectively, "I told you nothing would happen," and, "Now what you gonna do?" In one of my junior classes that same week, I sent a student to the office for swearing, threatening, and using homophobic slurs toward another student. The student returned in fewer than 10 minutes—and entered my room saying, "I'm back, bitch." I immediately sent the student back to the office with another referral. A few minutes later, the assistant principal stormed into my classroom, with the student in tow, and yelled at me in front of the class, "Stop sending her to the office. You are a teacher. Do your job."

In one elementary school where I was consulting, an administrator and I watched a 4th-grader assault a teacher and destroy a room over a period of 15 minutes. The principal did not suspend him, because the student had been suspended multiple times before and was black, male, and special-ed—a demographic the principal had specifically been told by the district to reduce suspension numbers for. The next day, the same student threatened to rape and kill a female student at lunch.

In both of the above stories, the administrators might have handled the situations differently to create more beneficial outcomes. Just as some teachers struggle to handle discipline well, and sometimes take actions that make a situation worse rather than better, so do some administrators. This happens for various reasons. The administrator might lack training and/or experience. They might feel hemmed in by conflicting mandates or interests.

They might be overwhelmed by the number and frequency of behavioral referrals being written. Or they might just be having a bad day.

The first step toward change is simply to recognize that something needs to shift. These two stories of ineffective discipline are extreme situations and they are rare. But they do happen, as do any number of milder variations. When both teachers and administrators are willing to reflect honestly on their own actions, are open to hearing where they might have fallen short, and are seeking alternative solutions, then defenses come down, relationships improve, and community is built.

On the next couple of pages are three examples of the most common complaints that teachers express regarding office discipline, along with possible solutions. Do you recognize your school in any of these examples? Could any of the proposed solutions potentially be implemented at your school?

Food for Thought

The first step toward change is simply to recognize that something needs to shift.

Ineffective Office Discipline #1	Student is sent to the office where they then sit for some period of time, talk to no one, and are sent back to class.
Why it Might Happen	Nobody is available to talk to student. Admin or other support personnel are engaged in other job responsibilities or with other students or crises.
Likely Results	Student's respect for the school diminishes and behavior remains unchanged; teacher feels frustrated and unsupported.
Possible Solutions	Have more than one adult and/or location available where students can be sent when they cannot remain in class.

Ineffective Office Discipline #2	Student is sent to office where they talk with an administrator or a counselor, but the adult either: takes the student's word over the teacher's about what happened; undermines the teacher's reason for sending the student out; and/or commiserates with the student. Often student is sent back to class immediately.
Why it Might Happen	Lack of communication or positive connection between teacher and admin. Lack of professionalism on part of admin, teacher, or both. Admin frustrated with teacher's overuse of referrals or inability to deal with any but the most minor behavioral infractions in class.
Likely Results	Student's and admin's respect for the teacher diminishes; student's behavior remains unchanged and student feels empowered to act out more; teacher feels frustrated and unsupported.
Possible Solutions	Office adult empathizes without excusing the student's behavior and focuses on student's taking responsibility for their part in the interaction—even if they feel the student was provoked. Student does not return to class until they admit some responsibility and agree verbally or in writing to make an effort to have a more productive experience upon their return. Admin communicates with teacher about what transpired and supports teacher in brainstorming alternative disciplinary actions for future use.

Ineffective Office Discipline #3	Student is sent to office where they are given comfort and care, but no discipline or consequences.** ***Sometimes this is the correct action to take, especially in cases where the administrator has a stronger personal relationship with the student than the teacher or when admin is acting upon knowledge of bigger-picture issues the teacher might not be aware of. HOWEVER, it's included on this list because of its widespread overuse at some schools.*
Why it Might Happen	Admin not comfortable in the role of disciplinarian. Admin does not understand how consequences and behavioral learning are connected, or how appropriate discipline is used in the best interest of the student. Admin believes teacher is unintentionally provoking confrontations with certain students. Admin has a better personal relationship with the student than the teacher. Admin determines that greatest need for student is de-escalation rather than discipline. Admin is acting upon knowledge of bigger picture issues the teacher might not be aware of.
Likely Results	Being sent to the office becomes desirable. Student's behavior is unchanged. Teacher feels frustrated and unsupported. Admin feels frustrated or uncertain.
Possible Solutions	Admin makes a list of consequences at their disposal and establishes a progressive tracking system for individual students. Admin communicates to teacher what actions were taken with the student, and more importantly, why those actions were taken, within 24 hours of the incident. When appropriate, Admin shares any relevant bigger-picture issues the teacher might need to know about. Admin communicates with teacher about what transpired and supports teacher in brainstorming ways to positively connect with student in future.

Behavior problems in a school are not the fault of the administrators, just as behavioral problems in the classroom are not the fault of the teachers. However, administrators do set the tone for how schoolwide discipline will be handled, just as teachers set the tone for how classroom discipline will be handled. What we choose to do, and how we choose to do it, can make us part of the problem or part of the solution. When a clear, structured, and equitable system is in place and consistently followed by all, things improve.

> *"Behavior is what a person does,*
> *not what they think, feel or believe."*
>
> — EMILY DICKINSON, POET & AUTHOR

Begin with Data

Without data we are flying blind. Schoolwide behavior change takes enough work as it is. Rather than wasting our limited energy on perceived issues from limited observations, let's use it wisely by starting and ending with data.

An effective schoolwide discipline system will be built around what your data tells you about current behavioral problems in your school. You can't simply pull a plan off the shelf. It must be built around the school's specific set of needs. The school's needs will be evident in the school's behavioral data. This might include number and frequency of office referrals, suspensions and expulsions, staff anecdotal records and surveys, and current on-site observations. High referral counts should be examined in further detail to uncover patterns — in the types of offenses, the timing of offenses, and the students and teachers involved in the offenses. This data will help the staff to develop a clear understanding of where their efforts need to be focused. Wherever you put your effort is where you will see improvement. Everyone's time and energy is

A Closer Look

When a clear, structured, and equitable system is in place and consistently followed by all, things improve.

finite, so put your effort into the specific areas where you are experiencing the greatest challenges, and where that effort will return the greatest dividends.

Analyzing the data includes weighing different priorities, which are seen and reported through the lenses of staff with very different vantage points. For example, if a teacher is positioned well away from the office or is otherwise isolated, their picture of the behavior problems in a school is limited to what they see, literally. For example, if that teacher's room is adjacent to the bus-loading area, they might believe that bus referrals are an area of high need — because they see kids at the end of the day giving grief to a paraprofessional about procedures and routines. Although that particular duty assignment might require attention, the office could be receiving many more referrals from infractions happening at lunch, in the hallways, or before school. Another teacher might be acutely sensitive to students' use of profanity in class, even when it is not used maliciously or directed specifically at another person. As a result, this teacher has written multiple referrals for "inappropriate language" and sees this as a high-priority, schoolwide problem. However, few other teachers on campus have written referrals for profanity, and see much larger and more widespread problems occurring, such as students' verbally threatening their peers or teachers.

A Closer Look

Without data we are flying blind.

Straight Talk

You can't simply pull a plan off the shelf.

In addition to basing your system on data, your system must also be monitored using data. Perception of results isn't necessarily the same thing as actual results. By looking at the data over time, you can discern what real changes are occurring, where, and by whom. You can discern where change is not occurring and take steps to rectify that. Please note: although anecdotal observations can be acceptable pieces of evidence in determining whether or not change has led to success, these observations are vulnerable to being skewed by emotion. For example, the actions of an extreme student, whose needs are not being met by the system, can lead to multiple referrals — and the erroneous conclusion by some staff that the new system has failed. Data can combat such emotion-based conclusions. It can also prevent staff from overstating successes when the data shows otherwise.

From Scott

When I am working in a leadership position with a school in distress, one of the first things the staff and I will do together is look at data in very specific ways. For example, at one school where I was principal, we started by identifying that "classroom disruption" was the most frequent type of office discipline referral. So we looked at which grade levels and which teachers were referring on that the most. We also looked at the students involved, as well as what supports were available for both the teachers and the students. From there we were able to make strategic decisions about what needed to change and how. Our interventions included: providing coaching and training for some of the teachers around classroom discipline; revamping and clearly communicating to all staff the steps to be taken in class before sending students out; creating consensus around when and under what circumstances it was appropriate to send a student out immediately; providing clarity around how office referrals would be handled; and adding supports for some of the students, many of which are listed later in this chapter.

Food for Thought

Wherever you put your effort is where you will see improvement.

We also used year-over-year data to help us understand if our efforts in a particular area were being effective. At one time, fights at recess were a persistent problem. The school identified, taught, and practiced routines and procedures for the playground. We then found that most problems came from the same small group of students, who committed acts of physical aggression near the end of recess, during the transition to line up and return to class. These students were given "leveled recess." This meant that they had reduced recess time. Ten minutes before the end of recess, these students were collected and taken to the cafeteria, where they were supervised by certified or classified staff until the end of recess. The combination of leveled recess and re-teaching and practicing recess routines reduced fights at recess from more than 20 the previous school year to fewer than five in the year after implementation.

Schoolwide Support

Creating a system is a big bite to chew on. It requires many hours spent by many people who work together through multiple phases, including planning, training, initial implementation, reflection, revision, and secondary implementation. In this book, we focus primarily on the training and implementation phases of creating a system, especially those things that support Tier 3 kids.

Once you have examined your data and determined your areas of greatest need, consider some ways you can alter your existing schoolwide discipline system to better meet the needs of everyone. Include a specific focus on how to weave in multiple layers of support and intervention for your Tier 3 students. Agree on what will happen at each level of support. Be clear on the differences in what needs to happen when sending a referral for a relatively minor, episodic infraction versus sending a referral for an ongoing, major infraction. Discuss what you don't want to have happen and what you need to have happen so that everyone — student, teacher, and administration — feels supported. Find consensus.

Bright Idea

By looking at the data over time, you can discern what real changes are occurring, where, and by whom.

Below are some pieces that might be part of an effective schoolwide system of support for Tier 3 students. Consider if any of these are pieces that you might want to adopt or modify for your system, to support your most chronically challenging students.

The Puzzle Pieces of Intervention

Imagine that a challenging Tier 3 student is being hugely disruptive to the class and the learning within it. The teacher has made three or more attempts, using consequences from multiple levels on their hierarchy, to redirect the student or to control the disruption, without sending the student out of class (see Chapter 3 for how teachers do this). Nothing has worked. The teacher has determined that the best next step is for the student to leave the room for a period of time. But where will the teacher send them?

Bright Idea

Ideally, when a student is sent out of class, the teacher can select from among several destinations.

Ideally, when a student is sent out of class, the teacher can select from among several destinations, depending on the type, severity, and regularity of the behavioral infraction. In each of these places, the student will have the opportunity to calm down, reflect, and reset before returning to class. Sometimes this transition will be quick and informal, and sometimes it will take a chunk of time and be more involved. Below are some out-of-class interventions that your school might consider adopting, as appropriate.

Buddy Room

The teacher sends the disruptive student to another teacher's classroom. This might include the student's taking their work, completing it in the other teacher's room, and then returning. Or it might involve taking a behavior-reflection sheet to fill out and then return; see samples of behavior reflection sheets in Appendix D. When a student returns from the Buddy Room, have them sit and quietly begin on some work until you have a free moment to debrief with them privately. This debrief can be as simple as taking their reflection sheet, skimming it, and giving them a thumbs up, or saying "welcome back" in a sincere voice, or dropping a sticky note on their desk telling them you're ready for a better time together and hope they are, too. Or the debrief can be as elaborate as taking a couple of minutes to verbally review their behavior or reflection sheet and set collaborative goals. The most important thing is to provide a clean slate, and try to move forward productively together. Things to think about:

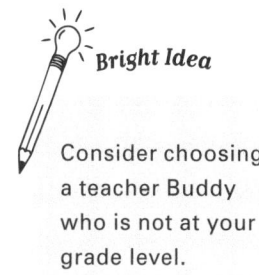

Bright Idea

Consider choosing a teacher Buddy who is not at your grade level.

▲ Consider choosing a teacher Buddy who is not at your grade level. Sending students to another teacher in your grade level can be problematic. If the student knows some of the other students in the Buddy Room, they might attempt to engage or distract their friends.

▲ Choosing a Buddy is not necessarily a quid-pro-quo arrangement. In some schools, one teacher might provide the Buddy Room for several other teachers — and some teachers won't be the Buddy Room for anyone else. Make choices based on what you think will work best for kids.

Trusted Adult

The teacher sends the student to another adult in the school to debrief and reset. Trusted Adults are usually assigned as part of a structured Behavior Intervention Plan (BIP). The student does not have to be in special education or have an Individualized Education Plan (IEP) to be put on a behavior plan. Any student with extreme behavioral needs can be selected for additional support, and a plan can be created to support them. The Trusted Adult can be any adult on campus, certified or classified, that the student feels positively connected to. The role of the Trusted Adult is not to give the student hugs and cuddles, or to let them escape responsibility for their actions by commiserating with them and taking their side over the teacher's. The role of the Trusted Adult is to listen, empathize, help the student take responsibility for their part in any confrontation that occurred, and then reset before they return to class. See Chapter 5 for more on individual behavior plans and how Trusted Adults are chosen and utilized.

In-School Intervention (ISI) Room

The teacher sends the student to the ISI Room. ISI Rooms go by different names in different schools, but their goal is to be a place where students can progress through the 5 Rs of behavioral support.

The 5 Rs are a method for teaching behavioral lessons after a major behavioral infraction has occurred. It allows the student to calm down, receive emotional or behavioral support, reflect on their behavior, and return to class better prepared to learn. **The 5 Rs are:**

- ▲ Release (emotionally purge negative feelings)
- ▲ Recover (generate internal calm through a mindfulness practice)
- ▲ Reflect (discuss and dissect what happened)
- ▲ Reset (set behavioral/emotional goals and/or practice coping mechanisms)
- ▲ Return (prepare an apology and/or positive intent and return to class)

An ISI Room is best staffed by a full-time, classified staff member with a background in psychology or behavior intervention. However, it can be successfully run by others, too, such as a teacher on special assignment with a background in behavior intervention or a paraprofessional who just has a knack for working with volatile kids. When the 5 Rs are done well, a student will be in the ISI Room approximately 30 minutes. Sometimes, depending on the student and the infraction, they might stay longer.

A Closer Look

The 5 Rs are a method for teaching behavioral lessons after a major behavioral infraction has occurred.

RELEASE: Students sent to the ISI Room almost always enter upset. The first goal is to allow them to release that upset and cool down on their own. For example, there might be three different areas/tables/desks in the ISI Room from which students can choose

The 5 R's of Intervention

RELEASE
- physically purge negative emotions
- mangle, squeeze, or stretch pliable object, punch pillow, scribble in notebook

RECOVER
- generate internal calm
- deep breathing, stretching, guided meditation

REFLECT
- discuss what happened
- consider triggers, options, responsibility

RESET
- set goals
- practice coping techniques

RETURN
- prepare apology or positive intention
- return to class

CLEAN SLATE
- teacher welcomes student back
- teacher accepts apology or positive intent
- teacher offers student clean slate

to quietly cool down. Each area might include a different kind of seating or various tools to interact with — something to draw or write on; flexible objects to mangle, squeeze, or physically manipulate; soft things to hit or to cuddle. No matter where they decide to sit and start, the student always follows a very specific entry routine. Generally this routine includes entering, placing their referral in a specific location, sitting at a cool-down area, and remaining there in relative silence until the ISI teacher approaches and indicates that it's time to transition to the next R, Recover.

RECOVER: Once the student has cooled down, they do a 5-to-10-minute physical recovery activity. Now that the student has achieved external calm, we want them to find internal calm before we do a verbal debrief with them. Physical recovery activities, or mindfulness practices, might include deep breathing, stretching, or meditating. These activities allow the residual upset and anxiety still in the student's body to dissipate. Ideally, students choose one of these to do on their own. To assist older students who have never done this before, a binder can provide simple, clear instructions for how to do each activity. With younger students, the ISI teacher will have to guide them through one of these activities the first few times they come to ISI. Over time, however, even younger students learn to do them on their own. In some schools, special computer programs lead students through breathing exercises or guided meditation. Students sit with a tablet or computer and select a mindfulness exercise from an online list. They listen through headphones and are guided through the practice on their own. See Appendix A for recovery techniques and resources.

> ☀ *Bright Idea*
>
> Physical recovery activities, or mindfulness practices, might include deep breathing, stretching, or meditating. A binder can provide simple, clear instructions for how to do each activity.

REFLECT: After physically recovering their internal equilibrium, the student will verbally debrief what happened, one-on-one with the ISI teacher. There are two goals for this debrief. The first goal is to discern what triggered the student's behavior and how it escalated to the point where the student was sent out of the room. The second goal is to have the student recognize their part in what happened and take responsibility for it. See Appendix A for reflection techniques and resources.

RESET: Once the student and the ISI teacher have talked about what happened, how it happened, and why it happened, then the ISI teacher will work with the student in setting a behavioral goal for returning to class and/or practice a coping mechanism with the student. Coping mechanisms might include anger management, anxiety management, or social skills-development techniques. The reset ends with the student's making a commitment to try to have a better day or behave differently in class. If a student cannot commit to try, then they're not sent back to class and might be sent to the principal instead for further intervention. See Appendix A for reset techniques and resources.

▲ **Bright Idea**

If the student isn't sincerely sorry, they could take a note reading, "I'm calm. I'm ready to try again".

RETURN: The student will return to class with a written apology or statement of intent to have a better day. This should be authentic and sincere. If the student isn't sincerely sorry, then they should not bring a note reading, "I'm sorry." They could, however, take a note reading, "I'm calm. I'm ready to try again," for example. Once a student returns to class, they have a clean slate. *Note that a clean slate simply means that the teacher treats the student like any other student in class. If the teacher is holding onto any residual, internal upset of their own, they will often unintentionally provoke another confrontation with the student.* The ISI teacher calls home after the student returns to class to inform the parents of the steps taken to help the student, and logs the incident so that the administration is also aware of what happened.

Things to think about:

▲ Students can be sent to the ISI Room more than once in a day. But generally, if they have been to the ISI and then continue the same misbehavior when they return, they would then move on to the administration. If the behavior is different, or the same but still relatively minor, they might end up in the ISI Room again. These are judgment calls that can only be made by the teacher at the time of the disruptions. In addition, principals can refer students to the ISI Room if they believe that a student who was sent directly to the office would be better served in ISI.

▲ The ISI teacher can send students to the office for administrative intervention if the student cannot successfully be redirected to an attitude appropriate for return to the classroom—or, at the secondary level, if the student has been sent to ISI by several different teachers throughout the day.

▲ Every visit to the ISI Room ends with the ISI teacher's completing an incident log report. A student's first visit always ends with a phone call home. Successive visits might or might not include parent contact, depending on the circumstances.

▲ The ISI teacher often ends up building strong personal relationships with the most troubled students in the school. This positive relationship can be deepened when the ISI teacher does monthly celebrations with students who reduce their visits to the ISI Room over time.

▲ The selection/hiring of a qualified person to run the ISI Room is absolutely essential to the success of the system. Ideally this would be a psychologist, behavior specialist, or some equivalent—but in the end, what matters most is not the person's credentials, but their skill in working with tough kids during emotional crises.

▲ In many cases, an administrator, Trusted Adult, counselor, security officer, nurse, or other adult on campus might find themselves in the position of supporting a student in crisis. When the ISI Room is full, or there isn't an ISI Room, then any adult pressed into service to support a volatile student can use informal versions of the 5 Rs. With brief training, any adult can simply say:

  • "Have a seat and try to calm down for minute. Here's some water."

  • "Let's take some deep breaths together,"
    or "Let's go for a short walk."

  • "Tell me what happened."

  • "If this same situation comes up again with your

teacher, what can you do differently so you do not end up sent out of class?"

- "Let's get ready to return to class. What can you say to your teacher to show them that you are ready to be back in the room? Do you want to take them a note or tell them with your voice?"

Office Referral

The teacher sends the student to the office to talk with an administrator. Receiving an administrative referral should be something all kids seek to avoid, not because the administrative team is cruel and capricious, but because the administrative team is firm and no-nonsense. Being sent to the office cannot be something that students look forward to, see as a treat or a break from the hard work of learning, or even just interpret as nothing to be concerned about. When this happens, the administration has ceased to be part of the solution. Moreover, it's unintentionally undermining the school's discipline system and the behavioral growth of the student. It's hard to be the heavy, but someone has to do it. Discipline can be done with a tender heart, but it cannot be done without a backbone.

Just like teachers, administrators should have a clear set of flexible, leveled consequences that they consistently draw from when students are sent to the office. These consequences, and how they are generally applied, should be clearly communicated to the teaching staff. Common consequences given by administrators include, but are not limited to:

- ▲ Stern talking-to.
- ▲ Phone call home.
- ▲ Recess or lunch detention.
- ▲ After-school detention.

Bright Idea

When the ISI Room is full, any adult pressed into service to support a volatile student can use informal versions of the 5 Rs.

Food for Thought

Receiving an administrative referral should be something all kids seek to avoid.

- ▲ Campus clean-up, during recess, lunch, or after school.

- ▲ Reflection sheet.

- ▲ Letter of apology to teacher.

- ▲ In-school suspension, from a single period in secondary or a single learning block in elementary.

- ▲ Visit to Buddy Room to complete work.

- ▲ Overnight suspension, in which the student cannot return to school the next day unless parents come with the student for an intake meeting with the principal.

- ▲ Short-term (1 – 5 days) out-of-school suspension.

- ▲ Long-term (6 – 19 days) out-of-school suspension.

- ▲ Parent conference.

- ▲ Loss of privilege, such as being banned from participating or attending a school-sponsored event, activity, or trip.

- ▲ Recess/lunch restriction, in which the student is allowed to attend first half of recess or lunch, but is removed from their peer group before the break ends. Younger students might be escorted to class one-on-one before the rest of the students begin to line up. Older students might report to the office 10 minutes before the end of lunch to check in, and then be escorted or sent to their class before the first bell rings, or with a pass after the second bell rings.

- ▲ Referral to other services or supports the school has in place, such as ISI, restorative justice, counseling, or student study team.

Many administrators use a progressive, discipline-tracking system to track how often certain students visit the office. Having a clear tracking system can help them decide what the most appropriate consequence is in any given interaction and help them to make it clear to the student what will happen the next time they are sent to the office.

Referral Policies

Every school needs a clear referral policy that's set up to support both students and teachers. If your school currently has a "no referrals" policy or a restricted policy, such as "no referrals unless the student is being a danger to self or others," then we strongly recommend that you change the policy. These types of policies undermine behavioral learning and create resentment among staff.

There are generally three reasons an administration might create a restricted referral policy, as outlined in the chart below.

Straight Talk

Discipline can be done with a tender heart, but it cannot be done without a backbone.

Reason	Argument Against	Alternative Solution
Administrator under district pressure to lower referral and suspension statistics overall, or for a specific demographic.	Letting statistics—and district directives based on those statistics—block doing what is right for students and the school allows chaos to thrive and undermines discipline and morale.	Use data to identify inequities in referrals, share this data with teachers, and brainstorm solutions. Train teachers to recognize their own biases and to use equitable de-escalation techniques. In the meantime, continue to allow referrals and to suspend students where warranted.
"No referrals" policy created to curtail its overuse by certain teachers.	Micromanaging an entire staff, when only a few teachers need intervention, undermines discipline and morale.	Meet monthly with teachers who overuse referrals. Show them data comparing their use versus the average use for the rest of the staff. Brainstorm solutions and practice de-escalation techniques together. In the meantime, continue to allow referrals as necessary and where warranted.

Reason	Argument Against	Alternative Solution
No administrator consistently on-site because administrator is being shared by more than one school site or is off-site for a training or to fulfill other responsibilities.	Having no out-of-classroom adult that teachers can use for support when necessary undermines discipline and morale.	Create a list of other adults on campus to whom teachers can send disruptive students in emergencies, when no administrator is available. Distribute list to all. Discuss how and when to utilize it and what to do when no adult is available or when situations become dangerous.

At any school with a chronically high referral rate, you will find one or both of the following circumstances to be true. Most of the referrals come from the same, small handful of teachers, and/or most of the referrals are about the same, small handful of students. Trying to solve this by telling all teachers to not write referrals is like telling an entire class that they have detention because the same three kids keep misbehaving. It punishes everyone for the inadequacies of a few and creates widespread resentment. It also removes a necessary level of consequence that even the most effective teachers need to have at their disposal. Trying to find a middle ground by telling an entire staff not to write referrals "unless it's for physical violence or verbal threats," for example, mitigates this problem to some degree. But limiting the reasons why referrals can be written to something so discrete and specific still ties the hands of teachers who might be working with chronically challenging students—students with underlying issues that manifest in the classroom as escalating disruption and defiance.

Talking back, refusing to follow directions, distracting others, and showing disrespect are not in and of themselves behaviors that warrant referrals. However, when multiple, appropriate efforts are made to redirect a student and the student nonetheless continues to be an overwhelming distraction to the learning of others, then sending them out is an appropriate response. If a teacher can't refer them under these circumstances, then the student learns that there is only so much the teacher can do. Once the teacher has exhausted what they can do, then the student actually can behave however they want without further recourse. This is antithetical to behavioral learning.

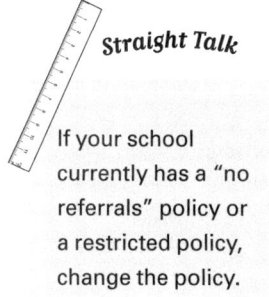

Straight Talk

If your school currently has a "no referrals" policy or a restricted policy, change the policy.

One Size Doesn't Fit All

Schoolwide systems and supports should not be rigid. They should be flexible and adaptive. For example, some Tier 3 students might be sent to ISI multiple times over the course of a day, because their impulse control and/or emotional issues are overwhelming them in waves—but they are not sent to the administration. In other cases, a student might be sent directly to the administration, bypassing smaller interventions such as the Buddy Room, because their behavior has become physically dangerous.

With Tier 3 students who have extreme and chronic behavioral issues, being sent to ISI is about intervention. It's about resetting, emotional skill-building, and creating another chance for the student to return to class and have a productive day. On the other hand, being sent to an administrator usually indicates that they are out of chances.

This differs from working with Tier 2 students, in that students with slightly less extreme or less chronic behaviors generally respond productively to receiving a firm consequence from the principal. That is, the consequence given in the office is uncomfortable enough that they change their behavior, at least temporarily, as a result. Tier 3 students, on the other hand, often do not change their behavior upon receiving an administrative consequence, and therefore require a different type of intervention. There is still a limit, though, to what Tier 3 kids can be allowed to do, and

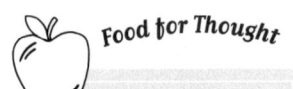

Schoolwide systems and supports should be flexible and adaptive.

how often they can be allowed to do it. At some point, an administrative consequence, such as out-of-school suspension, must be applied.

All students are different, and their misbehavior needs to be handled based on what works for them, what their needs are, and what will ultimately help them to learn to make better choices. Although this means that consequences will not necessarily be applied in exactly the same way with all students, it is still "equitable" in that it is responsive to individual needs and situations, and is always applied to achieve the greatest good.

EQUALITY   EQUITY

Disproportionality

Trying to create equity in the application of consequences is much trickier than it seems. Disproportionality in suspension rates has been a plague afflicting schools across the country for decades. Students of color, especially African-American males, are suspended at a much higher rate than their White counterparts. Our call for differentiation in the application of consequences must be coupled with an understanding of the prevalence of historical injustices in this area.

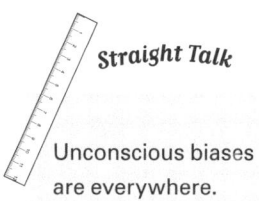

Straight Talk

Unconscious biases are everywhere.

Unconscious biases are everywhere, and they are notoriously difficult to break, because they are, by definition, invisible to the perpetrator. Data, systems, and mind-sets can help. Disaggregate the suspension and referral data at your school. As a staff, examine trends. Honestly discuss the changes that need to be made to improve behavioral outcomes for ALL students, especially for those populations that are, or have been, marginalized. Hold every student tenderly in your heart. Adopt a standardized, progressive system for applying and tracking administrative consequences.

We must be vigilant in our attempts to expose and extinguish existing biases. When students of one race are given fewer chances or more severe consequences, then that is racism-based decision-making. When students with extreme behavioral issues are given alternate activities or more therapeutic consequences, then that is equity-based decision-making. The difference lies in the what and the why. Ask yourself: Would you give this

Bright Idea

Adopt a standardized, progressive system for applying and tracking administrative consequences.

consequence to any student — every student — who came to the office on this referral? If you would not, then is this alternative consequence meant to help or hurt? Is it meant to holistically support a larger-than-normal need, or is it meant to be punitive and painful?

The Importance of Commonality

Using a common language and a common set of expectations might be the most important component of successfully maintaining an effective schoolwide discipline system. When an adult speaks to a student or group of students about expectations and discipline, then the language needs to match what those same students have been taught at the beginning of the school year, and what they're hearing from other adults. When all adults on a campus are using the same language to reinforce the same set of behavioral expectations, then the number and frequency of student violations diminishes. When a teacher chooses to function apart from the rest of the school, then their students are more likely to resist corrective discipline by other adults and these students are less equipped to follow the norms of the school. See Chapter 6 for more on leading schoolwide change and creating staff buy-in.

A Closer Look

> When all adults on a campus are using the same language to reinforce the same set of behavioral expectations, student violations diminish.

As students progress through the grade levels within the school, as they move from classroom to classroom, classroom to specialists, and classroom to common areas, they must not be met by significant variance in language or expectations. If they do, then preventable confusion and frustration result.

Secondary Scenario:

Mr. Smith: Johnny, take out your ear buds and put your phone away.

Johnny: But Ms. Jones lets us use headphones and listen to our music while we work!

Mr. Smith: I am not Ms. Jones. The school policy is no ear buds. Put them away.

Johnny: Why can't I use them? I work better when I listen to music.

Mr. Smith: Johnny, you can put them away now, and all is well, or we can step outside and see if we can resolve this privately. Or maybe you need to talk to an administrator about it. What do you want to do?

Johnny: Fine! *(Muttering loudly.)* A**hole.

Mr. Smith: Johnny, go to the office.

Even though Mr. Smith handled the situation calmly and clearly, without cornering Johnny, Johnny still ended up in the office. But this was an avoidable, teacher-created interaction. If Ms. Jones had been following the agreed-upon policy, then Johnny would probably not have resisted Mr. Smith's attempt to enforce it.

Elementary Scenario:

Cafeteria Maven: Sally, come here and pick up this trash you left behind.

Sally: *(Pretends to not hear and continues walking away.)*

Cafeteria Maven: Sally! I know you hear me. Get over here and pick up your trash!

Sally: *(Turns and glares at Cafeteria Maven.)*

Cafeteria Maven: Get! Over! Here! Now!

Sally: *(Crosses her arms, throws out her hip, and rolls her eyes.)*

Cafeteria Maven: You will not roll your eyes at me! Go to the office!

In this case there are likely two adult inconsistencies at play that led, at least in part, to Sally's being sent to the office. The first is that Sally believes that it's okay to ignore adults, not respond, and use less-than-respectful nonverbal body language. She is learning that this is acceptable in her classroom, where her teacher routinely allows or ignores this type of behavior. The other issue in this scenario is that Cafeteria Maven is not following the agreed-upon, schoolwide system for intervening with students when they're resisting or being defiant. What adults have been requested to do is stay calm, use a soft and kind voice, and offer the student a choice, such as, "Sally, you can come pick up your trash and then go to recess, or you can go to the office and miss your recess today. It's up to you. If you have not started picking up the garbage in 10 seconds, then I will write you a referral to the office." Then the adult is supposed to walk away. This is a de-escalation technique, discussed in detail in Chapter 3, that this school had adopted. Would Sally have then picked up the garbage? We don't know. But was it more likely she would pick up the garbage and less likely she would end up in the office? Yes.

On a campus where a common language is used consistently to implement a common system of discipline, students learn quickly where the boundaries are. That does not mean they won't step over those boundaries on occasion, but it does reduce the number of students who step over, and the frequency with which they do it.

Establishing Commonality

Common language around a common discipline system can be established in three main ways. You can adopt a pre-created system; you can modify your existing system with the help of a consultant to give your staff some concepts, strategies, and language to start with; or you can create your own system from scratch. Each of these has pros and cons, as presented in the chart on page 127.

Slow But Steady

Schoolwide systems, like anything else, take time to find their footing. Initially, a new system is almost always limited in its implementation, inconsistently utilized by staff, and heavily tested by both students and teachers. This testing will quickly expose the holes in the system — but more importantly will expose the school's commitment, or lack thereof, to making it work.

A Closer Look

Be patient when, in the beginning, referrals increase as teachers learn to navigate the new system and students test its limits.

You need to find the right combination of patience and pressure for your students and staff in developing and implementing a schoolwide system. Staff need to know what is expected of them, be supported and trained, and then be held accountable for their part.

System Type	Pros	Cons
Adopt a Pre-Made System	Low initial time commitment. The system, its components, training materials, and support resources are already created. Common language already exists and is built into the system. Other schools across the country might have also adopted the system, and their experiences can be drawn upon to help with implementation and overcoming roadblocks. Expert trainers in the system might be available to help with all levels of implementation over time.	Low staff buy-in, teachers might feel that they had no say in creating the system, and/or might feel the system is not desirable/appropriate for the school or for them. The system might not fit your exact needs and/or might be incompatible with things that you already have in place and that are already working. Can be very expensive if trainers are brought in to teach staff the system and support them with implementation.
Bring in a Short-Term Consultant	Low initial time commitment. Consultant can provide one or just a few days of training over the year. Common language already exists and is built into the training. Staff can pick and choose which concepts and strategies from the training best fit the school and students, and best fit into existing systems that are already in place and working. Medium to high staff buy-in. Moderate financial commitment.	Supporting research, resources, and materials might be limited. Other schools basing their discipline systems off the consultant's training might be few and far between. Time must be spent as a staff. agreeing on what to keep, change, add, or get rid of from the existing system.
Build Your Own System	High staff buy-in. Total flexibility in what the system will look like and how it will work. Costs nothing.	Many meetings required over the entire year to plan, draft, and revise the system. No pre-existing common language. No supporting research, materials, or resources.

You can't expect them to be perfect, and you can't let them pretend that no system is in place. You have to use professional judgment in applying what is needed, and when. And you have to be patient when, in the beginning, referrals increase as teachers learn to navigate the new system and students test its limits. Students also need to be trained on the new schoolwide plan. They then need the pressure of expectations, re-teaching, and positive and negative consequences to find success. And they need the adults to be patient with them as they learn what might be a significantly different way of behaving within your school.

A Closer Look

Expect to give your new or altered system three years of focused and committed effort before seeing significant success.

Schoolwide change is a long-term game. Plan to meet as an entire staff at least four times in each year, and much more frequently in smaller teams. In these meetings, debrief how it's going, look at data, share successes, discuss roadblocks, and brainstorm potential modifications. Most importantly, don't give up after Year 1, even if Year 1 is chaotic and only creates limited positive results. Year 1 is for experimenting, adjusting, finding small successes to build upon, creating excitement — or even just familiarity — and identifying teacher leaders who can help persuade their more reluctant colleagues to get on board in Year 2. Expect to give your new or altered system three years of focused and committed effort before seeing significant success worth writing home about.

▲ ▲ ▲

Yeah Buts & What Ifs...

Teacher: What if a student refuses to leave the room?

When a disruptive student refuses to leave the room, then the teacher calls for help. Initially, this call goes out to the adults on campus who have the most authority, such as the principal or a campus security officer. However, most schools also have multiple other adults who do not have full-time teaching or supervision duties, and who can be pressed into helping in a pinch. This might include the family liaison coordinator, on-site mentors, literacy or math coaches, or teachers on special assignment working in other capacities on campus. Who on the campus of your school does not have a classroom and can be engaged, when necessary, to help escort a student to the office when admin or security is unavailable?

Teacher: What if a student refuses to leave the room AND is being physically violent?

When a student is being physically violent—a danger to self or others—and won't leave the room, then the teacher calls for emergency support from the administration or campus security. Together, the staff will use de-escalation techniques to remove any triggers, redirect the focus of the student, and end the aggression. For the safety of the rest of the class, it's often best to simply have the teacher remove everyone else from the setting. This takes the audience away from the violent student and lowers the number of possible victims. The next step might be to change the arrangement of the classroom, to prevent self-harm and harm to staff. This can mean moving chairs, tables, desks, and other obstacles out of an area, and preventing the student from having access to material with which to continue to take out their aggression. If staff presence and verbal de-

Bright Idea

When a student is being physically violent, it's often best to simply have the teacher remove everyone else from the setting.

escalation do not end the physical violence, then staff might need to begin appropriate physical restraints**. The purpose of any physical restraint is to end the threat of harm to the student and any other people in the area. Restraints should only be done by people who have been trained and certified in child restraint and should be applied in the quickest possible manner that results in the end of the physical aggression without harming the student.

**Physical Restraint

Restraining of students, whether in special education or general education, is a serious and widely debated topic across the country. Federal, state, and local laws all might come into play when considering the restraint of a physically aggressive and violent student. Staff should always know what their district policies are regarding physically restraining students. Keeping yourself safe and employed are both legitimate goals when deciding what your role is in any situation where you might have to physically interact with a violent student.

Straight Talk

A child allowed to destroy a room until they calm down on their own learns that there are no boundaries, and that any behavior will be tolerated.

Although physical restraint should be used only as a last resort, and only by staff who are trained and certified in safe restraint methods, in some cases it is not only necessary—it is what the student needs. A student who is physically destroying a room is likely crying out to be restrained. They cannot control their own actions and need outside control. The student's underlying need is containment, and when they are restrained appropriately, they learn several important facts. They learn that the school setting has behavioral lines that cannot be crossed, and that adults on campus care enough about them to teach them where these lines are. A child allowed to destroy a room until they calm down on their own learns that there are no boundaries, and that any behavior will be tolerated. Because they are learning the wrong behavioral lesson, they will ultimately repeat this behavior until someone does step in and indicates otherwise, through both words and actions.

Unfortunately, physical restraint in schools is being widely misused. According to an analysis done by the Education Week Research Center, in the last year that complete statistics were available, more than 200,000 incidents of physical restraint involving special education students occurred in the United States. Some of these ended in children being assaulted and injured.

Bills have been introduced in multiple states to further limit the use of restraint for special-education students. These bills are a reaction to the misuse of the techniques. On the flip side, a 2017 bill in Nebraska sought to do the exact opposite; it would have expanded both the ability of school personnel to apply physical restraint and the legal protections for doing so. Thousands of Nebraska educators wrote to their unions in favor of the bill. Although neither the union nor any other educational organization in the state officially endorsed it, and it never made it to a vote in the state legislature, this speaks to the nature of the controversy. Teachers in schools working with high-need, at-risk student populations are experiencing extreme defiance and sometimes violent behaviors from children and teens on a daily basis, yet they feel helpless to do anything about it. On the other hand, some students are being physically abused by the overzealous application of physical restraint techniques. So, while physical restraint can and is being used to dominate and harm children in some places, it's also being used to contain and protect them in others. In still other areas, it's not being applied at all, to the detriment of the student, their class, their teacher, and their school.

Administrator: What if we can't afford an ISI teacher?

There is never enough money to go around. Finding the money to fund a new position, such as an ISI teacher, is always fraught with difficulty. There are different ways that funds might be acquired or freed up for this use, but as with all budget-related decisions, applying money to one area means not applying it to others. Consequently, funding an ISI position first has to be a priority for the school. Once it has been established as a priority, then an existing non-instructional staff position might be cut in order to make funds available. Alternately, federal program money or grants might be acquired to fund the position.

Administrator: What if the ISI Room fills up?

Even in the roughest of elementary schools currently utilizing ISI Rooms, it's rare for more than three kids to be in the ISI Room at any one time—even in a school with an average of 500 students. On a day of crisis, you might have as many as 10. Middle and high schools averaging 1,000 students would rarely have more than five or six in ISI at once. If you find you have more than that, inconsistencies and other sources of confusion probably need to be resolved in other parts of the schoolwide or classroom discipline systems.

Meet with the teachers who are sending students to ISI the most frequently and debrief the interactions that led to the referrals. Discuss modifications and alternatives, if the opportunity presents itself. Teachers might be erroneously sending Tier 2 students to ISI for relatively minor infractions, when those students would have been better served by being sent directly to the office. ISI is for students who are chronically explosive, aggressive, defiant, disruptive, or shut down, and with whom the standard application of classroom and office consequences has been tried multiple times, in multiple ways, with little to no effect upon the students' behavior.

The ISI Room might fill up initially, as you work out the kinks in the system, or occasionally on particularly rough days. One option to consider is occasionally adding extra support, as required. If the ISI teacher requests support, or an administrator or another non-classroom

Straight Talk

When all hands are needed on deck during a perfect storm of schoolwide chaos, then everyone—regardless of job description—needs to pitch in.

teacher notices that there are a lot of students in the ISI Room, then they should jump in to help. They can pull individual students out, do the best they can to work through the 5 Rs with them, and transition them back to class. When all hands are needed on deck during a perfect storm of schoolwide chaos, then everyone — regardless of job description — needs to pitch in to support one another and the students.

Teacher: What if we have a "no referrals" or "no sending students out of class" policy?

A detailed answer to this question is covered in the *"Referral Policies"* section earlier in this chapter.

Teacher: What if none of this works?

If none of the classroom or schoolwide supports in this book is working to create change in a Tier 3 student's behavior, it's probably time to try a one-on-one intervention (see Chapter 5). When even that doesn't work, it might be time to consider connecting them with supports outside of the school and/or transferring the student to an alternative therapeutic or educational environment.

Teacher: What if my administration isn't supportive/helpful?

As discussed in the chart at the beginning of this chapter, teachers often feel that the administration isn't supporting them. This is most likely when they send students out, only to have them return a few minutes later — often with no change in attitude, or with an attitude of vindication rather than remorse. When teachers sense that this is happening, it's time to have a conversation as a staff. Agreed-upon understandings about the concepts and techniques discussed throughout this chapter are critical; they allow everyone to find consensus and then implement changes. We are all on the same side and want what is best for kids and their growth. When administration and staff have an adversarial relationship, everyone loses. The best way to get on the same page and feel supported is through regular communication and willingness on everyone's part to hear and understand where others are coming from. When we all take responsibility for ourselves, admit when and where we have fallen short, and keep our hearts and minds open, then we can find ways to move forward. Flexibility, assuming the best about one another, regular communication, and clearly defined systems can turn an adversarial relationship into a productive one.

Administrator: What if teachers are not making necessary changes in their own behaviors?

If we are assuming the best, then we can assume that every adult wants to improve their ability to successfully support kids, both emotionally and academically. Admitting that what you are doing now isn't working is hard. And even if you recognize the disconnect, and are willing to admit it, trying new things that do not come naturally is even harder. As the building leader, you need to be supportive and patient. "Supportive" means giving your teachers the tools and training they need to change or improve, time to practice and master new skills, and opportunities to reflect together with their peers. "Patient" means allowing teachers the space to try just one new thing at a time, and understanding that trying and failing is part of the process, to be expected, and even to be celebrated. The only unacceptable approach is refusing to try anything at all.

One of the most powerful ways to support teacher reflection and growth is through peer observations and video recording. You have exceptional teachers in the building right now. Are you benefiting from them? Are other teachers, paraprofessionals, kitchen staff, office staff, and custodians getting a chance to see them in action? Peer observations are a safe, positive way

Straight Talk

When administration and staff have an adversarial relationship, everyone loses.

to spread the excellence in one room into as many as you can. Video recording allows a teacher to observe themselves in action as well. Our brains are marvelous at altering perception and remembering things the way we wanted them to be, instead of the way they were. You say to yourself, I used soft eyes and soft voice, but it didn't work. But did you? Let's go to the video and see! Such a safe method for self-evaluation can be a game-changer for staff. Keep in mind that video recording is about watching the teaching and reflecting on what the teacher said and did. It is not about watching kids after the fact, trying to catch them at being off-task.

Food for Thought

Trying and failing is part of the process, to be expected, and even to be celebrated. The only unacceptable approach is refusing to try.

▲ ▲ ▲

Summary & Applications

- ▲ Referrals are a consequence that teachers need to have at their disposal. Administrators should avoid blanket "no referrals" policies.

- ▲ Data is your friend. Let data inform your practice, decisions, and solutions regarding how and where to support Tier 3 students.

- ▲ Having an ISI Room, or some equivalent behavior-intervention location, where students can be sent for support rather than for punishment, is a necessity when working on a campus with a large number of Tier 3 students.

- ▲ Multiple support people and locations — such as an ISI Room, Trusted Adult, and Buddy Room — increase the probability that students who are exploding or imploding will find success at school.

- ▲ Ineffective office discipline comes in various forms, but there are solutions. Honest and open communication between staff and administration is key.

- ▲ Unconscious biases around student discipline are pervasive and must be unearthed and addressed honestly.

- ▲ Having common expectations and common language around behavior and discipline — consistently used by all staff — leads to faster and more sustainable changes.

- ▲ Schoolwide change is a long-term game. You didn't find yourself in need overnight. You won't come out of it overnight.

Discuss

▲ What do you like or appreciate about how office referrals are handled at your school? What do you dislike or wish was different about how office referrals are handled?

▲ How many referrals do you typically write in a year? What kinds of infractions and/or with what types of kids are these usually written? Can you identify a discernible pattern that might help you to make strategic decisions about where you want/need support? For example, are most of your referrals written at a particular time of day or for a particular gender, race, personality type, or behavior?

▲ Do you use Buddy Rooms or Trusted Adults at your school to support the needs of Tier 3 students? If you do, how are they working, and how might they be improved as interventions? If you don't, would one or both of them be worth trying? Why or why not?

▲ Does your school already have common language, common expectations, and common techniques that all staff are expected to use to de-escalate volatile situations with kids? If so, how are all staff being trained and supported around them? How are they being held accountable for consistent implementation? If not, how might it aid your school to establish these, and how might you start?

▲ Does your school have common data gathering expectations for teachers and common planning time built into the schedule? If not, how might these types of routines be established?

Apply

▲ Review your referral policy as a staff; be sure to involve all teachers, administrators, and support staff. Decide together on revisions to the policy that would better meet the needs of both staff and students.

▲ Staff an ISI Room and decide on the process and procedures that will be used in it.

▲ Review schoolwide behavioral data and look for trends, patterns, and the big issues that need to be addressed.

▲ Choose Buddies for Buddy Rooms and decide how they will be used.

▲ Decide on a common set of behavioral expectations for kids, teachers, and administrators, and adopt a common language around its use.

▲ Research and acquire the tools, resources, and trainings that your staff will need in order to better meet the needs of your Tier 3 students. Focus on learning and practicing various de-escalation techniques and socio-emotional intervention strategies.

▲ Review the "Ineffective Office Discipline" examples at the beginning of this chapter. Assess honestly which scenarios are true of your own school and discuss solutions.

▲ Create and share a list of all consequences an administrator might give. Decide how consequences will be applied in a progressive way with students who visit the office frequently.

▲ Have a discussion or do a book study on identifying biases. See additional resources in Appendix C.

▲ Create and distribute to all staff an "escort list" of all the people on campus who can be contacted to escort a student out of class when the need for removal arises. Put the list in priority order, with contact information for each person.

5

ONE-ON-ONE INTERVENTIONS

"Breaking a habit really means establishing a new habit."

— TIMOTHY PYCHYL,
PROFESSOR OF PSYCHOLOGY

I N THIS CHAPTER, WE OFFER POSSIBLE SOLUTIONS, for when nothing else works. Maybe you have faithfully implemented the classroom and schoolwide structures in the previous chapters in this book. You have assumed the best, conducted private conversations, built personal connections, delivered mild, moderate, or extreme consequences, and applied socio-emotional interventions — and nothing seems to make any difference in a particular student's behavior. In this case, the student might need a different kind of support. Tailored, one-on-one interventions are sometimes the answer. These types of interventions are time-, energy-, and labor-intensive, but often can help Tier 3 kids to replace chronic negative or unproductive behavioral patterns with more productive ones.

▲ ▲ ▲

Reflect First, Act Second

Before considering one-on-one intervention, reflect on the following questions:

- ▲ Have I tried a half-dozen or more different consequences with the student?

- ▲ Have I been giving consequences with love in my heart and softness in my eyes?

- ▲ Have I been offering the student behavioral choices and using the language of choice?

- ▲ Have I attempted to find out what their interests are, and then taken time to chat with them about those interests over a period of weeks, in an effort to positively connect with them?

- ▲ Have I been in regular contact with the student's parents?

- ▲ Have I been in regular conversation with an administrator or support-provider about the student and my attempts to help them?

- ▲ Have I been working with the ISI teacher, special-ed teacher, or other in-building support staff involved with this student?

- ▲ Have I been doing all of the above for at least a month?
- ▲ Do I honestly believe it is my job to help this student to improve their behavior?
- ▲ Do I honestly believe this student can be helped by me, even if the other adults in their life are not supporting my efforts?

If you answered "no" to any one of the above questions, try working on that first.

Change is Hard

Think of a bad habit or addiction that you suffer from — one you would like to stop, have tried to stop multiple times, but keep going back to. Perhaps you habitually overeat, smoke, swear, text while driving, procrastinate, bite your nails, or show up late.

From Grace

When I was in college, I was habitually sarcastic. I didn't realize how often I used sarcasm, because I had grown up in a very sarcastic household. That's just how we talked. I thought that's how everyone normally communicated. But during a college party, an older friend of mine took me aside and said to me, "Gracie, nobody likes it when you're sarcastic. It's mean and ugly. You gotta knock it off or tone it down, or people aren't gonna want to be around you." I was devastated. And defensive. I went through the five stages of grief. Stage one is denial. "Okay. Sure. I'm sarcastic all the time. Right. Got it," I said sarcastically. Over the next week I felt angry, then depressed. Then I had a moment of clarity and acceptance. When I was calm and really thought about it, I knew that my friend was right. I was sarcastic A LOT. Upon reflection, I could see why people wouldn't really like that.

So I decided to stop. I went to bed that night, woke up the next morning, and was never sarcastic again. Ha! No. That didn't happen. I wanted it to happen, though. I wanted to wake up and never be sarcastic again. But it isn't that simple to break a chronic or habitual behavior, even when you want to.

So what does this have to do with Tier 3 kids? Tier 3 kids present with the most extreme examples of chronically negative behaviors in the classroom. Yet we tend to pull them aside and say things to them like, "Just stop doing that." Or, "Just be like this instead of how you're being." But they can't, because change isn't that simple.

Changing a chronic behavior is like trying to change a habit. Wait, it is changing a habit. To create a new habit, one has to have a replacement behavior in mind and then practice the replacement behavior — the new, different, or more appropriate behavior — for at least 30 days. That's the minimum, not the average or the maximum. That's the best-case scenario. Building better habits or behaviors is not an all-or-nothing game. It's an ongoing, sometimes gradual process. When working with Tier 3 students to create replacement behaviors and habits, you are often in for a long, slow, and difficult process. The amount of time and practice it takes before a new behavior becomes automatic can vary widely depending on the behavior, the person, and the situation. It includes fits and starts, backsliding, and big feelings. It requires an enormous amount of support, patience, and love — from you.

Straight Talk

It isn't simple to break a chronic or habitual behavior, even when you want to.

"Longtime habits are literally entrenched at the neural level...It's much easier to start doing something new than to stop doing something habitual...."

— ELLIOT BERKMAN, PROFESSOR OF
PSYCHOLOGY AND NEUROSCIENCE

Swaddling Interventions

When newborn babies get emotionally triggered or upset, they cannot calm themselves. Swaddling—snugly wrapping a baby in a blanket—is a common way to provide the security and warmth the baby needs to calm down. When used in combination with other interventions, such as bouncing and shushing and giving them something to suck on, swaddling is one of the most efficient and effective ways to calm an outraged infant. The beautiful thing about swaddling is that it's firm but soft at the same time. It allows the infant to wiggle and push and fight and express their frustration, while still holding them safely and softly within a clear boundary. This is why "swaddling" makes for an excellent metaphor for how to design an effective one-on-one intervention plan with students exhibiting Tier 3 behaviors. In a literal swaddle, the boundary is the blanket and the reinforcement comes from the tightness with which it's wrapped around the infant. In a metaphorical swaddle, the boundary is a stated behavioral norm that the student needs to follow, and the reinforcement comes from the consequences and incentives attached to following it.

A Closer Look

Changing a chronic behavior begins with choosing and practicing a replacement behavior for a minimum of 30 days.

The goal of a "swaddle intervention" is to create a structured behavioral plan in which a student can struggle but still be held accountable, as they attempt to change their behavior. Just as a literal swaddle involves two people, a parent and a child, a swaddle intervention involves two people, a teacher and a student. A variation of the swaddle intervention, called the "village intervention," includes multiple adults and is used when a swaddle intervention proves to be ineffective. The village intervention will be described later in this chapter.

Swaddle intervention plans, although in some ways similar to IEPs and BIPs, are significantly different from these more traditional intervention plans in critical ways. The most important differences are that swaddle plans always focus on breaking only a single, discrete behavior over a long period of time—and the student will have some say in what the plan looks like. Also, everything in a swaddle plan will be observable and trackable. Finally, and perhaps most importantly, a swaddle plan includes the teacher's committing to their own behavioral changes as well.

In Appendix B, we have included some sample elementary and secondary swaddle interventions that were run successfully with real students. You also will find some blank planning guides and templates to help you to create your first swaddle intervention. But first, below are descriptions and explanations of the four phases.

A Closer Look

Swaddle plans always focus on altering only a single, discrete behavior over a long period of time.

Effective behavioral boundaries are like a swaddling blanket in that they are simultaneously firm and flexible.

Swaddle Phase 1: Pre-Planning

Before meeting with the student about the intervention, find out if they have an IEP, a 504 Plan, or any other support plan or services already in place. If so, know what each of these supports is and what accommodations, modifications, or resources it specifies. Next, rough out a possible plan of support that eventually will be suitable to share with the student. Decide on what accommodations you want to try, how you will track them, and what incentives you might offer to help the student to buy in. These are all just rough ideas, though. Nothing is written in stone at this point, as much of it will likely change once the student is brought into the conversation. Pre-planning will include:

1. **Assume the best.** As discussed in Chapter 2, misbehavior can be perceived as disrespect and disinterest, or it can be perceived as a request for help. Choose to perceive it as a request for help. Consider what the Invisible Subtitle might be for the student. This is essential in setting the right tone for your interactions with the student and establishing a dynamic that's most likely to succeed.

2. **Choose a single focus.** The student might have demonstrated multiple behaviors that need changing, but asking them to change more than one at a time is unrealistic and a set-up for failure. Initially, limit your focus to only one of their unproductive behaviors, and let the others go. Choose a behavior that the student can realistically address, one that if addressed, will immediately provide them with a sense of accomplishment. For example, put their focus on coming quietly into class and sitting in their assigned seat, even if they still come in late and unprepared. Or focus on their removing themselves to a specific location in the classroom when they get upset, even if they still explode, grumble, and are disruptive all the way there and after they arrive.

   ▲ **Be realistic.** You are not likely to see overnight change if you ask a blurter to stop calling out, a wanderer to stop getting up from their seat, or a volatile student to stop being explosive and confrontational. Your intervention plan has to begin with a small, realistic "stepping-stone goal" that is totally achievable in the first day or week. Over a series of weeks, you move toward larger and larger goals, until you reach an acceptable new behavior. But in the beginning, start small. If the student can't taste success in the first few days, they will never really buy into the process.

Straight Talk

Asking a student to change more than one behavior at a time is unrealistic and a set-up for failure.

▲ **Be concrete.** Make sure you choose something observable and trackable. Making the goal "Be respectful to adults," or "Follow directions" is too vague. A more specific goal might be "Comply without verbal comment when asked to take out materials," or "Move without speaking when asked to sit in a specific place."

Here is a list of common behaviors that Tier 3 swaddle interventions might focus on:

- Not yelling at/threatening/intimidating peers.

- Remaining in seat during direct instruction.

- Remaining in seat during independent work.

- Complying with simple requests, without arguing.

- Staying in the classroom unless given permission to leave.

- Not hitting/biting/pushing/touching others.

- Raising hand to answer questions or ask for help, instead of blurting.

- Not talking while the teacher is talking.

- Staying silently on task for 10 minutes or more.

- Entering room quietly and getting immediately to work.

3. **Create a preliminary plan.**

▲ **Outline a rough plan.** Decide what accommodations can be made to help the student to reduce a negative behavior and practice a replacement behavior. Create short- and long-term goals. Keep them specific and achievable. Decide on a series of possible incentives you might offer and how they'll be both earned and tracked. The most important thing is to have a series of stepping-stone goals that over time get more difficult, or require more from the student, until ultimately a replacement behavior has been established. The initial goal cannot be to achieve the replacement behavior. That's the ultimate goal. The student needs smaller, easier, stepping-stone goals to achieve on the way there.

▲ **Create a tracking system.** Think explicitly about how you want to track the student's progress and how they will be able to earn rewards. Will you have a chart on their desk where they self-track their successes and failures? Or will you have them track only successes? Or will you be tracking the information yourself? How can you make this simple and easy?

▲ **Create consequences.** Supporting a student in creating a replacement behavior does not mean that they are now free to misbehave without consequence. Support requires care and structure, but it also requires boundaries. It requires consequences for crossing those boundaries. However, the consequences you use during an intervention might be different from those you typically use, or you might apply them differently. For example, if an ongoing, disruptive, or unacceptable behavior usually results in your taking recess away or assigning detention, then during the intervention plan you might choose a different consequence. Or you might modify your use of the consequence by having the student work with you during recess, lunch, or after school. The focus of the "revised detention" would be to work with you on their intervention plan and practice their replacement behavior, instead of just having them sit in silence or complete academic work.

▲ **Choose incentives.** Decide on some incentives that might work to help motivate the student and reward them for their efforts. Make sure you have some ideas for both small and large incentives, so you can stagger them and attach larger incentives to larger successes as time goes on. The first incentive should be attached to a simple, short-term goal. This is usually something that lasts less than a school day, and often less than a class period—and it should earn the student a small incentive on the first day, if possible. Incentives only work if students can taste them, and thus begin to internalize the connection between their choices and the fruits that follow.

A Closer Look

Your intervention plan has to begin with a small, realistic "stepping-stone goal" that is totally achievable in the first day or week.

▲ **You change, too.** Think about how you will support the student in following the plan and what you intend to do differently as part of that support. Remember: kids don't change until adults change first. For example, you might make one or more of the following commitments:

- I won't yell at you or raise my voice with you.

- I will use nonverbal signals to redirect your behavior or remind you to follow the intervention plan.

- I won't keep you in at recess or assign you to lunch detention.

- I will provide you with all necessary materials in class.

- I won't assign you homework.

- I will check in with you daily to champion your progress and set goals for the next day.

- I won't ignore you or your disruptive behavior.

- I will stay calm and kind when redirecting your behavior or giving you a consequence.

- I will always offer you an explicit choice to follow my instructions or receive a specific consequence, before giving you that consequence.

- I won't give up on you, or the plan, even when we have a bad day.

- I will remind you that bad days and small failures are all part of the process, and they don't mean that we aren't making progress.

Swaddle Phase 2: Share the Plan

Once you have a rough plan worked out, meet privately with the student to share it. This meeting might also include another adult, such as the principal or a special-ed teacher, depending on the situation and your relationship with the student. Get the student's input and ultimately their commitment. This phase includes:

▲ **Share the plan with the student.** Start by expressing concern — for the student as a human being, rather than the student's performance or progress in school. Invite their feedback on the request (replacement behavior), the supports (accommodations that will help), the tracking system, the incentives, the consequences, and the ways in which you will change. Be open and ready to make reasonable alterations to any or all of these based on the student's input.

▲ **Commit to trying the plan for one week.** Be explicit with the student about how you will support them in following the plan for the first week, how you will be tracking it, how they earn their first reward, and what you will be doing differently that week, as well. Get them to commit to try. If you can't get them to acknowledge that they will try, then assume the best, read the Invisible Subtitle, and move forward. For example, to the student who remains silent or belligerently says things like, "You can do whatever you want, I don't care," you can respond with, "Even though you haven't said you're ready to try, I believe we can make this work. I care too much about you to let things continue the way they are. So we will start tomorrow. I'm looking forward to it."

 **A Closer Look**

The consequences you use during an intervention might be different from those you typically use, or you might apply them differently.

▲ **Practice together.** If the student is not completely shut down, then practice or role-play some scenarios where they would need to follow the plan. Go through the motions with them, and try to get them to "play their part." Be sure you have created total clarity. If they are too resistant to role-play with you, then you can model for them the wrong way and right way to follow the plan. They might pretend to not watch or listen. That's okay. Trust that it's helping anyway.

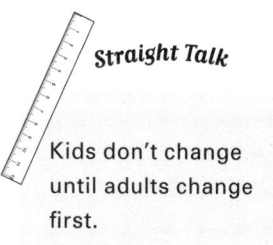

Straight Talk

Kids don't change until adults change first.

Swaddle Phase 3: Implementation

Put the plan into effect in real time in the classroom for one week.

▲ **Set the stage for success.** Catch the student at the beginning of class on Day 1 of the intervention to remind them of the plan. Tell them that you are on their side and excited to make a first attempt with them.

▲ **Debrief every day if possible.** The student needs ongoing feedback about how they are doing. After tracking their behavior as agreed, share and debrief with them daily, if possible, even if it's just a one-minute conversation at the end of the period (secondary) or after recess/lunch and again at the end of the day (elementary). Or, maybe provide a note that acknowledges successes and challenges, and optimistically sets the goal for the next day. Keep these conversations and/or communications light and positive!

▲ **Give rewards immediately.** As the student reaches the first stepping-stone goal, provide them with their first reward on the spot. If at all possible, make their first goal so simple that they could receive a small reward the first or second day.

▲ **Don't punish kids when they struggle.** Breaking a chronic behavior is tough. At first, you might see some real progress as the extra attention and the earning of small rewards gives the student a boost of motivation. But there will also be

Bright Idea

When running an intervention, debrief with the student daily, even if it's just a one-minute conversation.

bad days, or days when the newness has worn off, and the student needs to know that this is to be expected. They need to know that fluctuations in performance are normal, okay with you, and don't mean they have failed or that they can't get back on track. If they act out on a bad day and end up with a consequence, be sure to debrief later. Offer a clean slate and your renewed support. Alternately, kids might initially resist the intervention and end up in the office or even suspended from class — some do this multiple times in the first and second weeks. This does not mean the intervention isn't working. Again, it is incredibly difficult to change a habitual behavior. Some kids cannot do it immediately. Some need to feel the sting of the new consequences before they believe that you are serious about following the plan and holding them accountable, especially if you have not consistently held them accountable for the behavior in the past. FYI: Letting it be okay that a student fails sometimes does NOT mean letting them get away with disruptive behavior. It means holding them consistently accountable in a firm but gentle way, while simultaneously, encouraging them to work toward the replacement behavior. It means not getting upset, not blaming the student, and not giving up.

Swaddle Phase 4: Reflection, Revision, & Re-Commitment

▲ **Reflect and revise the plan.** After the first week, review with the student what progress has been made. Daily check-ins can be as small as just catching their eye and giving them a thumbs up for the day. But weekly debriefs should include a private sit-down to make alterations for greater success, discuss roadblocks to success, or celebrate existing successes. Ask the student how they think the plan is working. Be open to making revisions based on their feedback and/or your experience. Create clarity about how the plan will be implemented in the next week, especially if any modifications are being made. If you make changes to the plan, then practice together again. Be sure that the student knows what you're asking them to do. Be sure that you understand what the student is asking you to do. Be clear about what changes you expect before they can earn rewards. Depending on how the first week went, you might make the plan easier or harder. Stay positive, even if the first week was rough. It's all part of the process.

▲ **Re-commit for another week.** Thank the student for their efforts, no matter how small. Without blame, share where you feel challenged. Speak from a place of care and kindness, and keep it brief. Just a few sentences. "This was a hard week for me. It was hard for me to see you struggle and also to hold you accountable when you went too far. But I know it was in your best interest, and I feel good about what we're trying to do together." Verbally commit to trying again the following week. Just as before, try to get a verbal or physical commitment from the student. If they resist, fall back on your positive assumptions about them and the process. You might say, "I know this week was hard for you. But I'm proud of the small success you had, and I'm looking forward to next week." Or, "I know it felt like nothing went better this week and our plan isn't working. But change is hard and takes time, and everybody learns at different speeds. I know we will get there. I'm looking forward to trying again next week."

A Closer Look

Stay positive, even if the first week was rough.

▲ **Plan for six weeks.** Chronic, inappropriate behaviors are often unconscious coping mechanisms that have developed over time in reaction to ongoing traumatic experiences or environments. Making a change, even one for the "better," involves giving up the behaviors that have served to self-protect and self-soothe. Consequently, the student most likely will go back to those behaviors, at least sometimes in

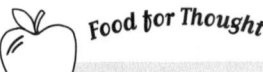

the beginning, when self-soothing and protection are needed. That's one reason why it takes time to change those behaviors, and why "backsliding" is so common. You won't see a steady ascent to success. You will see peaks and valleys. Make peace with this. Commit to six weeks for this swaddle intervention, with weekly debriefs, daily check-ins, and ongoing revisions.

▲ **Consistently implement the plan.** This is often the hardest part of these types of interventions. It is time-consuming and exhausting to check in with the student daily and weekly for an entire month or more, champion their progress, reset when they backslide, stay on their side, change our own beliefs and reactions, and create space for them to fail — all as they make their first fledgling steps toward trying out a new behavior. On the other hand, without putting in the time — without consistent implementation — even an excellent plan will fail, no matter how well-crafted it is.

Informal Swaddling

It is not always necessary to make the one-on-one swaddle intervention process as formal as the description above, or as demonstrated in the example plans provided in Appendix B. The concept of the swaddle intervention can be applied more informally, and it might even work better that way in some cases. Sometimes it might be enough just to meet with the student, discuss the problem, decide on a possible solution, and choose an incentive. Then, just go for it. In this informal plan, you don't fill in any forms, but you monitor the student's progress throughout each day and check in with them as you go along, adjusting when it seems necessary.

From Grace

I was recently told by an elementary teacher that she had a 2nd-grade student who was constantly wiggling and wandering and flopping and invading other people's spaces. It was extremely distracting, but not malicious. He wasn't defiant or confrontational; he just had very low impulse control. Nonetheless, he was constantly getting in trouble for not listening, not following directions, not doing work, and disturbing others. She decided to try an informal, one-on-one swaddle intervention that was loosely based on an intervention she had heard me describe in my Conscious Classroom Management training.

She met with her student and told him they were going to work together to help him to become his best self, learn faster and better, and get in trouble less often. She put five sticky notes on the side of her white board. She created a new protocol: Every time he had to be told twice in a row to stop doing something, he would walk to the white board, remove a sticky note, place it on her filing cabinet instead, and then return to his work. If he had at least one sticky note remaining on the white board at the end of any day, then on that day he would receive a reward. She brought in a tube filled with small dinosaur toys that he coveted. When he won a reward, he could choose a dinosaur from the tube. This is how the plan played out: If he rolled around on the carpet, then she would give him a warning and tell him to sit up and pay attention. If he rolled around again in the next 10 minutes, then she would point to the board and he would walk over, move one sticky note, return to the carpet, and attempt to alter his behavior. By the third week of

Bright Idea

Try a simple, informal version of a swaddle intervention. This is often enough to help a student create change.

the intervention, he was receiving a dinosaur almost every day, and his focus, behavior, and work all had dramatically improved.

I once had an 8th-grader who displayed many disruptive behaviors. One, which commonly occurred during whole-class discussions, was to blurt out whenever another student was answering a question. She would talk over the other student, screeching her own opinions about either the topic or about what an idiot the other student was. Her blurts often included profanity, as well. I met with her after school and told her we needed to find a less disruptive way for her to express herself during class. I showed her where I had placed a special binder at the back of the classroom for her to use. I told her that when she started blurting out, I would say her name once, to get her attention, and point to the binder. Then, her job was to stop talking, walk to the binder, write out whatever it was she wanted to say to the class — or to the other student, or to me — and then return silently to her desk. For every successful trip to the binder, I gave her a $1 coupon for the student store. By the fourth week, she was earning multiple coupons every day — so I made it harder to earn them. Now, a $1 coupon was earned only when she actually didn't blurt out at all, or started but stopped herself immediately. She learned to get up and write in the binder without my having to remind her. After another two weeks, I was able to remove the incentive and the intervention altogether. She kept her own notebook open during class discussions, so she could write or draw out her comments as class discussions took place.

Sometimes, informal swaddles are enough. Generally speaking, however, informal swaddles work best with two specific groups of kids. They work with Tier 2 kids who have been misidentified as

Tier 3, and they work with Tier 3 kids whose behaviors are chronic and disruptive, but not belligerent, confrontational, or volatile. With Tier 3 students who are also aggressive or explosive, a more formal intervention process generally works better.

Village Interventions

Sometimes, swaddling a baby is not enough to calm them. When a baby cannot be calmed by intensive swaddling, coupled with other supports, then the parent might need outside help from another caregiver or even a doctor. Likewise, when a swaddle intervention is having either no or limited success after four or more weeks of implementation, then the teacher needs outside help. This is when we move from the swaddle intervention to the village intervention. Village interventions are essentially just a more intense and in-depth version of swaddling. This type of plan includes multiple, additional people in support of the teacher and the student. A village intervention follows the same process as the swaddle intervention, but also includes several additional elements, as described below.

A Closer Look

When a swaddle intervention is having either no or limited success, we move to the village intervention.

In Phase 1: While pre-planning, widen the net. **Collect and analyze any existing data.** Look at the student's file, test scores, record of referrals, suspensions, detentions, and arrests. Talk with their current and past teachers, parents or guardians, counselor, social worker, group-home liaison, and anyone else who might have information or insights that might help you to understand the student better. Look for information on both the student's needs and their challenges. Identify common misbehaviors and triggers. Also identify strengths, personal interests, and possible positive incentives.

If you are in a village intervention, you can assume there will be days and times when it will be in the student's, the class's, and the teacher's best interest to send the student out of class. Decide on what schoolwide and administrative supports can and will be provided on these occurrences. Who will they be sent to? What will happen to them once they get there? What needs to happen before the student can return to class? Under what circumstances would they not return to class?

In Phase 2: When you share the plan, **circle the wagons**. Share the plan with the student, as well as other teachers, administrators, parents or guardians, counselors, and other community or family members, as appropriate. Each person gets a chance to express concern and care for the student. In the process, the student gets a reality check: The "village," whatever its make-up for that student, sees them, cares for them, and has not given up on them. Ask the student what triggers their anger, upset, or apathy, and what can be done to minimize these triggers. Discuss what parts of their life they like the best. When, where, with whom, and doing what do they feel at ease, safe, comfortable, or happy?

Have the student **identify a Trusted Adult** who can be enlisted to help. This person can take on many possible roles in the intervention. This might be the person who:

- ▲ Receives the student when the student can't handle being in the room with their teacher.

- ▲ Drops in daily during the student's class to check in with them.

- ▲ Spends time with the student during "reward time."

- ▲ Assists the student with certain academic tasks — tasks the student can't seem to handle doing in class.

The Trusted Adult can be anyone on staff, another teacher, a paraprofessional, an administrator, an office staff person, a custodian, a literacy coach, a family liaison officer, a campus security officer. The student gets to choose this person. The Trusted Adult cannot be selected for them, because this is about personal connection. It is critical they choose someone they want to see for support. Although it's not ideal when they choose another busy classroom teacher, this is still preferable to having the Trusted Adult thrust upon them. Refer to Chapter 4 for more on the role of the Trusted Adult — which is not to condone or coddle, but rather to be empathic and supportive — and the 5 Rs. Trusted Adults help the student to take responsibility for their own choices and the effects of those choices, then help them to reset and return to class, more ready to focus and learn.

During Phase 3 and/or 4: As the implementation of a plan gets underway, try to connect the student with some **additional outside support**. If possible and appropriate, ensure that the student has access to psychological counseling. Tier 3 students often have a very low sense of self-esteem. Counter-intuitively, this sense can initially become magnified when other people share their caring and concern. The student might feel unworthy, or feel pain from trauma that might begin to surface. Having a professional on hand with whom the student can speak on a regular basis can sometimes make all the difference.

A Closer Look

The student gets to choose who they want as their Trusted Adult. This person cannot be chosen for them.

> ### From Grace
>
> Meet Kenesha. She was a student in my 10th-grade history class. Her mother was in prison and her father was deceased. She lived in a group home for teenage girls.
>
> About a month into the school year, and after threatening her history teacher and intimidating several students, Kenesha was transferred to my history class. On her first day, she walked in, ten minutes late, and announced, "Kenesha here now. Deal with it, bitches! Yah…you know you better watch yourself." When I asked her to step outside to have a private conversation with me, she replied, "Nuh-uh. I'm in this class. So now you got to deal." I again asked her to step out. She replied, "This is bullshit!" She stormed out and didn't come back until the next day.
>
> Kenesha's behavior didn't improve much over the first few weeks. Each day, she would pick a rule to break or an argument to have. When I calmly asked her to follow the rule, such as sitting in her seat or entering class quietly, she would curse and threaten, and eventually storm out of class.

I spoke with her social worker, her counselor, the assistant principal, and even tried a standard behavior plan. But with Kenesha, nothing worked. Not even a little. Not even for a little while. During this time, I remained calm on the outside. But inside I felt angry, helpless, and close to giving up on Kenesha. I found myself hoping that she would be absent, as I didn't want to have to face her storm.

Ultimately, I decided to assume the best about Kenesha. She needed help. I knew that her behaviors came from some unspeakable experiences that no child should ever have to go through. But I also wondered what kind of help a public school teacher could possibly provide to a student with a history of serious psychological and physical abuse, who is violent, unstable, oppositional, and intimidating.

I decided that while Kenesha was at the school and enrolled in my class, I would assume that she was reachable and teachable, but that she needed multiple layers of help from multiple adults in and out of school. She needed more than a standard behavioral contract. She needed an intense and wrap-around intervention involving multiple people and supports. She needed a Village Intervention. The intervention we put together for Kenesha started small. Our initial goal was just to get her to enter the room, whether late or on time, without talking. I just wanted her to come in quietly and sit in her assigned seat. That was it. More than a week passed before she accomplished this even one time.

During that first week, every time she came in talking, I indicated to Kenesha that she should stop and sit quietly. If she argued, I offered her the choice to sit quietly or go to her Trusted Adult to decompress. She chose the Trusted Adult every time, and never made it more than a few minutes in my classroom. But her Trusted Adult was also coaching her about her feelings; they discussed why she was having so much difficulty entering and sitting as requested. Sometimes she returned to class for a bit, later in the period. Sometimes not. But on

Day 8, she came in and sat down. She wasn't quiet or subtle about it, but she didn't speak. She made it halfway through the period before she stormed out to her Trusted Adult. The next day I dropped a note on her desk telling her how proud and happy I was to have her meet her first goal. I attached her reward, which was a $10 coupon for the school store. She pocketed the coupon, tore up the note, and made a show of throwing it away. But she then sat and quietly sulked for the rest of the period. She didn't do any work. But she stayed for the entire period and didn't disrupt! Another coupon was on her desk the next day, along with a note congratulating her on making her next reward. She was allowed to go to lunch 10 minutes early, with a friend of her choosing.

Over the next four weeks, we had good days and bad days. But the good days were slowly getting more frequent. About three weeks into the intervention, she contributed to a class discussion, and during the fourth week participated in classwork with a partner of her choice. Eight weeks after beginning, Kenesha came to class for five days in a row and sat in her assigned seat without interrupting my teaching or anyone else's learning. For that, she earned her biggest reward—a tour and a day-long visit at a local fashion college. At that point, we decided she was ready to change to a new goal of "completing assigned classwork." She didn't need to bring materials to class or complete homework. But since she was coming to class and sitting without disruption, and staying all period more and more frequently, we felt she might be able to handle a second goal, an academic goal.

A Closer Look

What seemed like inevitable expulsion was transformed as the "village" intervened on Kenesha's behalf.

While Kenesha continued to revisit her old behaviors occasionally, her attitude and conduct markedly improved overall. She felt safer, and was more able to touch an inner place where she could express that she did care, and did want to participate and learn. What seemed like inevitable expulsion was transformed, as the "village" intervened on her behalf.

Sample Interventions

In Appendix B, you will find blank swaddle intervention templates, along with a series of sample swaddle interventions from real teachers in some of the elementary and secondary schools where Grace has consulted. As you read through these, keep in mind that every intervention is unique. These samples are not meant to be used "as is" with your kids who have similar behaviors. Be ready, willing, and able to modify and adjust them to meet the specific needs of your students. For example, you might need to use different consequences or incentives,*** because the ones given in the samples might not fit your school or situation. That's okay; these are just samples. They worked where they were tried, but they are tied to their specific students, teachers, and contexts. The purpose of the samples is simply to clarify what this process might look like and how you might start.

Straight Talk

Sometimes you have to be willing to think outside the academic box in order to first meet a student's more pressing emotional, social, or behavioral need.

Also keep in mind that actual intervention plans are often not as detailed as the samples provided here. When you develop this kind of plan in your school, everyone involved will be intimately familiar with the context — what's happening with the community, school, and the student. We provided increased detail in these examples so that you can see parallels to your situation, and adapt accordingly.

*** In the village intervention story about Kenesha earlier in this chapter, and in the Appendix B swaddle intervention samples, you will see that early release from class and reduced homework were sometimes offered as incentives. We know that this is controversial. One might argue that offering these types of incentives sends a message to students that homework and/or class time are not important. We would argue, however, that sometimes you have to be willing to think outside the academic box and let go of what you — the adult — value in order to first meet a student's more pressing emotional, social, or behavioral need. Some students have bigger fish to fry than their academic progress. For some, class time and homework can be overwhelming and even trauma inducing. If the use of incentives that reduce time in class or academic work motivate a traumatized or behaviorally challenged student to buy in to an intervention and practice a replacement behavior, then, in our opinion, the reward outweighs the loss.

Why Interventions Often Fail

These types of interventions, while very time- and effort-intensive for teachers, can be very effective. However, they are more likely to fail when the teacher running the intervention does any of the following:

▲ Chooses too many things to work on with a student.

▲ Makes the initial "ask" too big—by asking the student to change too much, or asking for something the student can't realistically achieve at first.

▲ Does not involve the student in conversations about how the intervention will work and/or does not get the student's input, acknowledgement, or feedback.

Straight Talk

The teacher must be willing to change for the sake of the student's success.

▲ Removes support too quickly or gives up in the first few weeks.

▲ Does not regularly debrief with the student to reflect on successes and roadblocks to success.

▲ Does not give rewards when they are earned, on the same day or the beginning of the next day.

▲ Gives up on the process as a result of a rough/unsuccessful start or intermittent failures and backsliding.

▲ Is overly permissive and does not hold the student consistently accountable for inappropriate behavior.

▲ Is initially overly rigid, and therefore unwilling to coach and support the student.

▲ Is not assuming the best about their student.

▲ Is not willing to modify their way of being with the student. *If we keep doing what we are doing, we will keep getting what we are getting.* The teacher must be willing to change for the sake of the student's success. This almost always means being more structured, more clear, more reflective, more supportive, and more consistent with consequences.

▲ ▲ ▲

Yeah Buts & What Ifs...

Administrator: But what if a teacher says, "Why should this 'bad' kid get special attention and privileges?"

First, troubled kids aren't bad. They are hurt and suffering. If what we are doing isn't meeting their needs, then we need to do something different. That's our job — to give each student what they individually need in order to learn and thrive. Kids don't change until the adults change first. Second, they get special attention and privileges because they need them, and without them they, and we, will continue to suffer. Although one could argue that this isn't equality, it is equitable. Equal means doing for them what we do for all of our other students. Equitable means doing for them what they need to succeed, even if what they need is different from what our other students need. As teachers, we are in the business of being equitable, because stopping at equal leaves too many kids behind.

Food for Thought

Equitable means doing for one student what they need to succeed, even if what they need is different from what our other students need.

Teacher: But what if the student takes advantage of the intervention? For example, what if he gets up more than he really needs to because now it's "legal" to wander?

Students can manipulate or take advantage of the intervention only when the goal is too easy for them. Once you sense that this might be happening, then have a debriefing session in which you move them to the next stepping-stone goal—but leave the incentive where it is. In other words, start by making the same incentive harder to achieve. Maybe even jump forward two goals if you think it's necessary.

Teacher: But what if I don't have the time for this kind of intervention?

Time is relative. One could argue that nobody has the time for this kind of intervention. One could also argue that you are losing enormous amounts of time in dealing with the student, their off-task behaviors, and their disruptions to the class. If the student's behavior improves because of the intervention, then all the time you put into the intervention comes back to you tenfold. And you recoup much more than time; you'll have more energy and peace, as well.

Teacher: But what if the family is undermining the process?

While our assumption is that all parents try to act in the best interest of their children, there is little to nothing we can do when a dysfunctional family or parent is undermining the process, either consciously or unconsciously. When undermining happens, it's harder—but not impossible—for the student to achieve success. Kids learn very young that different adults have different expectations, and the kids are capable of altering their behaviors to meet those differing expectations. A child will act different with their permissive parent than with their stricter parent, just as they will act different with their various teachers. However, just as a family works more smoothly when both parents are on the same page about boundaries and discipline, our entire school environment works more smoothly when a child's family and the school are on the same page.

Sadly, when family is involved, we might not be able to get on the same page—but we still don't give up. We can still do what we can to make a difference in a child's life. We might lean on the serenity prayer, which advises having the strength to change the things we can, the courage to accept the things we can't, and the wisdom to know the difference. We can't change families, but we can change ourselves. We can help kids when we are willing to change for their benefit.

> **Teacher: But what if other kids notice or say it's unfair that an intervention kid has special privileges, different consequences, or unique resources?**

Some students will notice and comment on discrepancies in the resources or the discipline structures being used with other students. This is predictable, and it's reasonable that they might interpret this as unfair. When it comes up, be ready with answers. You might say something like, "Fair and equal are not the same thing. You are correct that I am not being equal, but I am being fair. My job is to make sure that each of you gets whatever you need to be as successful as you can be in school and life. What you need will be different from what others need, because you are all different people with different strengths and backgrounds. So you might see me doing things differently with others sometimes; that's because they need something different than you do to be successful. You will still get what you need, too."

Teacher: But what if the kid won't buy in?

When students refuse to buy in, assume that they want to, but simply cannot be vulnerable enough to admit it. That's okay. They're in a tough place. Go forward anyway. Really try to get them to comment on the incentives they'd like to earn and the things they'd like to see the teacher do differently. This might be met with an icy wall of "I don't care," and that's okay, too. Because they do care. Until they become able to express their care, we can care on their behalf and go forward with an intervention in good faith. Keep holding the door open for them to walk through. Go through the motions of the intervention, even if they stonewall. A student's exterior walls are protecting a mushy center. With enough effort and care, we can create tiny cracks in their walls and start to seep in there—even when those cracks are invisible to the naked eye.

Teacher: But what if the intervention doesn't make any difference?

When an intervention is run well—by people who believe in the child and in themselves, by people who are willing to change themselves to better support the child's needs—then the intervention will be successful on some level. However, it might not always seem or feel that way. Success isn't always immediately visible. The child doesn't always improve their behavior while they're with us. That doesn't mean we aren't making a difference to them. Sometimes kids need time and distance to internalize what people are doing to support them. Sometimes change built on that support takes time to manifest. But it does happen. Interventions are more likely to fail because of the adults involved—the beliefs they have, or the skills they lack, which subtly and often invisibly undermine the process—than because of the kids.

Food for Thought

Success isn't always immediately visible.

Teacher: But seriously, what if absolutely nothing works? Really, truly nothing. We are doing all the right things with all the right people in all the right ways. Now what?

Eventually, with some students, tough decisions need to be made about whether or not the school can realistically meet the student's emotional and behavioral needs. This is not common. Usually, changes to classroom and schoolwide systems, like those recommended in this book, can meet the needs of almost any student at some level. Still, sometimes it is in a student's and the school's best interest that the student is moved to a more restrictive or therapeutic environment. All districts have a process for this. These processes, which go by different names in different districts, all constitute a way to assess the student's need through some form of due diligence.

An efficient due-diligence process should take no more than three months to complete. Unfortunately, some districts are reluctant to support the process necessary to move a student to an alternative educational environment. This happens for many reasons, often historical, political, or economic. These reasons might include a lack of time and resources to complete the due diligence process, aversion to the bureaucratic red tape involved, lack of any alternate place within the district to send the student, fear of litigation and/or bad press, community pressure, lack of awareness surrounding what's really happening with the student at the school site, or historical baggage and prior abuses that need to be avoided. When this happens, the process stalls, sometimes taking more than a year to complete, while everyone suffers.

Students have the right to learn in the least-restrictive environment where their learning can be supported. But if a student is not only not learning, but is also derailing learning for others on a daily basis, then this is not the least-restrictive environment. This environment is not restrictive enough. When a school simply doesn't have enough personnel or resources to meet a student's needs, the least-restrictive environment in which they can be successful ceases to be the general school environment.

From Grace

I was recently consulting at a school where I witnessed a 1st-grader, let's call him Mikey, who ran through the hallways—screaming and opening doors to classrooms—while an adult ran after him, calling his name and trying to get him to come back. I found out later that the adult was his one-on-one aide. When the aide finally caught up to Mikey, Mikey threw his shoes at the aide and fell to the floor, squirming and screaming. When the aide attempted to pick him up and move him to a less public location than the hallway, Mikey kicked, hit, and bit him, and then ran down the hall. I asked the principal if this was a bad day for Mikey, or if this was his normal daily behavior. She said it was normal. I was shocked. What was he learning from being at school? Nothing academic, certainly.

Mikey was assigned to a 1st-grade class, and he started his day there. But he had never made it through more than the first 15 minutes of class without exploding into uncontrolled rampages and chaos, at which time he was removed by his aide to an empty conference room. There, the aide spent most of his day attempting to keep Mikey in the room—while simultaneously trying to avoid hurting either one of them or destroying the room. Mikey also spent some time in special ed, but he only made it for about 15 minutes, once or twice each day, before he had to be removed for uncontrollable behaviors. Mikey had a behavior plan, a special-ed teacher, and a one-on-one aide, but no interventions the school had tried had had any effect on his behavior. Kindergarten had been a disaster, and now the administration was in its second year trying, and failing, to meet Mikey's needs. They weren't failing because they weren't trying, or because they didn't have the knowledge or resources. They were failing because a standard public school environment was simply not the right placement for Mikey. At least not at that time.

A Closer Look

Mikey had a behavior plan, a special-ed teacher, and a one-on-one aide, but no interventions the school had tried had had any effect on his behavior.

When a student like Mikey is not in the right environment, his needs are not being met—but his are not the only needs that are not being met. Mikey caused chaos and disruptions that infringed on many other people. First, his behavior infringed on the ability of adults to do their jobs, who expended time and resources in monitoring and intervening, to no ultimate benefit. Second, his behavior also thwarted the learning in both his general-ed and special-ed classes, and greatly inhibited the access of other high-need students to extra support and resources. Even after he was removed from class, his classmates were left slightly traumatized and less able to focus and learn. Ultimately, the best course of action, for him and for everyone else, was to move him to an alternative educational environment where his needs might actually get met.

▲ ▲ ▲

Summary & Applications

Remember

- ▲ A Tier 3 student's extreme behaviors are a form of armor that protects them from an unsafe world.

- ▲ Changing a behavior is hard, takes time, and includes backsliding. Make peace with this.

- ▲ An effective intervention is metaphorically like a swaddling blanket. It establishes a clear boundary, but allows for testing and resistance without hurting the student in the process.

- ▲ Effective interventions focus on a single behavioral change. They are simple, realistic, concrete, trackable, and doable. And they include input from the student.

- ▲ Be willing to change your behavior, your expectations, and your use of consequences and incentives in order to support a Tier 3 student in making changes.

- ▲ Sometimes informal interventions are the best place to begin.

Discuss

- ▲ What are the possible advantages of using the swaddle model to support behavioral change — instead of a traditional BIP, or in conjunction with an IEP?

- ▲ Review the list of reasons why interventions fail. Do you recognize yourself in any of these? What can you do to avoid making these mistakes in your next intervention?

- ▲ What is in the way of your trying a swaddle intervention with a Tier 3 student? How can you overcome your resistance, whether internal or external, to trying one?

▲ Think of a Tier 3 student you have. What adult behaviors need to change in order to support a change in this student's behavior?

▲ Which adults in your building are already informal, go-to Trusted Adults? What about these specific adults attracts your most challenging students to them? How can these adults be used to support your swaddle and village interventions?

Apply

▲ Make a reference list of appropriate incentives that you could potentially offer to students as part of a swaddle intervention. You might consider incentives such as:

- Extra computer time
- Tangibles (stickers, food, or toys)
- "Cut-the-line" pass for lunch
- Tardy pass, homework pass, or extra bathroom pass
- Early dismissal (to lunch or at end of day or for a specific period)
- Coupons to campus store or cafeteria
- Free tickets to preferred school events (student dance, sports game, theatre show)
- Free yearbook or spirit wear
- Other???

▲ Make a list of the students in your class or school that would benefit the most from a swaddle intervention. Choose one to try a formal or informal swaddle with. Begin to pre-plan for a four-to-six-week process.

SECTION III —
Leadership

*Supporting Staff Through
the Change Process*

6

LEADING
THE CHANGE

> *"The effectiveness of a new culture depends on the strength of the people behind the change and the strength of the pre-existing culture."*
>
> — STEVE GREUNERT AND TODD WHITAKER,
> PROFESSORS OF EDUCATION

I N   T H I S   C H A P T E R ,   W E   W I L L   L O O K   A T   T H E   Q U A L I T I E S ,
techniques, and tools a good leader needs in order to create staff
buy-in and ultimately create sustainable change. It is not enough
to want your staff to change. Just as kids change when adults change
first, a staff changes when their principal or the administrative team
changes first. Just as reluctant students sometimes do best with a clear
plan to follow, a reluctant staff might need the same in order to make
changes in their attitudes and actions while working with Tier 3
students. Consider plans that include small, doable steps, incentives,
accountability, and ongoing reflection, modification, and support.
In the end, no plan succeeds, or succeeds for long, without honest
and respectful communication, trust, and a sense of communal
commitment and connection.

▲ ▲ ▲

Change is Possible

Creating positive behavioral outcomes in tough schools, and with
Tier 3 kids, is hard work. When facing a challenging behavioral
environment or situation — where success has been elusive, or when
the collective efficacy of the staff around behavioral improvement
is lacking — change is even more difficult. But that's
where we will start, with knowing and believing that
change is possible, that it has happened elsewhere,
and that the school you are currently in and the kids
you are currently working with are not exceptions
to the rule. Across the country, schools have had
similar challenges, issues, and roadblocks, yet have
still found a way to success. No single, struggling
school gets to receive the prize for "too difficult to
repair," nor does any single, struggling student get to receive the
prize for "too difficult to help." Positive change for your school or
students might not have happened yet, for what could be a myriad
of reasons, but it can. And it will.

Straight Talk

No single, struggling
school gets to receive
the prize for "too
difficult to repair."

The Role of the Principal

A principal can make or break a school site. Good teachers don't leave schools; they leave principals. Teachers will stay in difficult schools, with tough kids, no resources, and low pay when they feel supported by the principal. It is almost unheard of that a struggling school makes significant positive changes in climate, culture, or student achievement without a strong and capable principal. This isn't surprising. As in professional sports, no matter how many superstar players you have, without an effective coach, the team will not thrive or achieve its highest potential. Gifted players can achieve individually, but they can't win games on their own. They don't have the time, or sometimes even the skill set, to see the bigger picture, motivate the rest of the players, and create a game plan that leads to success for all. That's the coach's job. In a school, that's the principal's job.

Straight Talk

Good teachers don't leave schools; they leave principals.

No one is more important than the individual teacher to the success of positive behavioral outcomes for students. Teachers are the point-people for almost all behavioral interactions and interventions. However, administrators must take the lead in making both classroom and schoolwide classroom-management changes. Their expectations and support for student behavioral outcomes determine the path of the school. Their vision and big-picture strategy hold the plan together long enough for the changes to take.

From Grace

Before I transitioned into consulting, my last full-time job on a school campus was at a low-performing, high-poverty, urban high school in California, with almost 100 teachers and more than 2,000 students. For the 10 years before I worked there, the school's test-score-based Academic Progress Indicator (API) had flatlined in the mid 500s. An API of 800+ indicates a high-performing school. Anything under 700 shows a school in need. Anything under 600 is failing. My school was in academic crisis.

A principal who was also relatively new to the school had hired me to teach history and to run the school's professional development (PD). The PD that year was to be focused on literacy. Specifically, it was my job to teach the staff how to strategically teach reading comprehension within their individual subject areas. About half of the staff was not on board. The prevailing feeling among these staff members was that teaching teenagers how to read better was "not their job." Every department, even the English department, harbored significant resistance to this professional development. Even many of the teachers who saw the need for this type of PD were skeptical. They had all spent many years sitting through useless, flavor-of-the-month PD that went nowhere and did nothing to truly help them or their students.

As a staff, and as individuals, the teachers at this school on their own would not have chosen to focus their professional development on literacy. However, the principal was seeing the bigger picture and had identified the low reading ability of a majority of students to be a key stumbling block to their academic success. Remedial reading classes had been tried, but hadn't produced the desired effect. The remedial classes had only addressed the needs of the lowest-performing students, leaving unsupported a large, middle group of poor but functional readers.

A Closer Look

These teachers had all spent many years sitting through useless, flavor-of-the-month PD that went nowhere and did nothing to truly help them or their students.

So a new-ish principal brings in a new staff member to run PD with a large number of skeptical to outright-resistant teachers in a failing urban high school. Three years later, this school's API is almost 80 points higher. How did the principal do it? How did she get her reluctant staff on board?

1. She set aside three of the four calendared PD afternoons per month to be dedicated to staffwide professional development on content-based literacy instruction.

A Closer Look

> The principal was open to feedback, both good and bad. She was flexible. She supported good ideas, even if they weren't hers.

2. She hired a knowledgeable literacy trainer who had experience in working with similar populations of students, and partnered that trainer with an effective veteran teacher on staff who was well liked.

3. She worked closely with the literacy trainer to set realistic, concrete goals and timelines for staff training and implementation. She communicated these goals and timelines to staff. She made a three-year implementation plan. She designated Year 1 as a year of "learning and experimentation."

4. She made it clear that she was more interested in seeing teachers try new things and fail, than not to try anything new at all.

5. She held teachers accountable for trying and for acting professionally. She had ongoing, private conversations with teachers who were the most resistant. These folks fell into two main categories: those who were passive-aggressive and did not implement anything or bring requested student work to PD; and those who were aggressively undermining her plan, even trying to sabotage PD trainings or personally attacking me as I led PD meetings.

6. She attended the PD trainings and sat with teachers who were most likely to resist being productive.

7. She was open to feedback, good and bad. She was flexible. She supported good ideas, even if they weren't hers or weren't part of the original plan.

> 8. She found time and money to support extension work by anyone who was willing to jump in and take a leadership role.
>
> It was slow, grueling work to get the majority of the staff on board and trying new things in their classrooms, yet after three years of consistent effort, the improvement in the school's test scores made it the only school in the district to demonstrate any significant progress in test scores during that time period.

It's the administration's job to help the staff to see the problems that exist, and to plan for proactive changes to address those problems. The administration must also identify and strategically support new and struggling teachers. Just as teaching academics — such as reading and math — is based on a set of skills, so too is teaching behavior. Teachers receive minimal pre-service, classroom-management training, and what they have been taught might not fit the plan of the school or district. Although some might arrive with stronger relationship skills than others, it's hard for anyone to be prepared to have a 7- or 17-year-old curse them out for being asked to sit in their seat. Such events are rarely discussed as part of an undergraduate methods class. A new teacher's first response to being told where to place their head within their own body might not win any awards.

So how does an effective principal or administrative team support all teachers around behavior management? To begin with, struggling teachers who tend toward frustration, seething, yelling, and overreacting with difficult students need help. They need to be taught necessary

A Closer Look

Just as teaching academics—such as reading and math—is based on a set of skills, so too is teaching behavior.

skills, reminded of the process, celebrated for their successes, and supported through their failures, all while holding them to an expectation of change. On the other hand, proficient, balanced teachers who tend toward being simultaneously firm and soft—who hold difficult kids accountable while staying compassionate and maintaining positive relationships—need to be celebrated for their skill and groomed as leaders.

Effective Leadership—Dos & Don'ts

There is no greater barrier to creating positive change than the beliefs and dispositions of the school. If the adults working in the school believe that the current state of affairs is alterable, then improvement is possible. If they don't, then all the other ideas become significantly less likely to succeed. Everyone on staff, from custodians to main-office personnel, from teachers to administrators, must have faith that outcomes previously unseen are possible within the walls of the school. Students and schools coming from years of poverty, trauma, and academic failure can overcome these descriptors to find success. Other schools have done it. However, it can be difficult to convince an overwhelmed, resistant, or skeptical staff that those other schools are more similar to theirs than not—and more importantly, that the nuggets of wisdom learned in those other schools are keys to success in their own school.

Food for Thought

> Everyone on staff must have faith that outcomes previously unseen are possible.

From a leadership perspective, many practical moves, big and small, can be made to overcome resistance and build the collective efficacy of a reluctant staff. On the other hand, many things can also get in the way of building this collective efficacy. On the next page is a list of "Dos" that can help an administrator to build trust and motivation, and "Don'ts" that often work to destroy it.

DO	*DON'T*
▲ Value experimentation and effort over success, and show it.	▲ Criticize teachers or classified staff.
▲ Recognize your own mess-ups, make amends, and take steps to improve.	▲ Go too fast or expect too much change too quickly.
▲ Consistently ask for feedback.	▲ Refuse to apologize.
▲ Share and celebrate successes.	▲ Refuse to reflect on your own missteps and/or refuse to change based on staff feedback.
▲ Create positive personal connections with staff.	▲ Harp on failure and shortcomings.
▲ Have your office door open more than closed.	▲ Give criticism without compassion and support for making necessary changes.
▲ Respond to email within 24 hours.	▲ Show favoritism.
▲ Delegate. Use your support staff. Foster and trust teacher leaders.	▲ Focus too much on what's wrong, instead of on what's right.
▲ Attend, participate in, and/or lead staffwide PD meetings.	▲ Be overly rigid about policies or fail to allow for reasonable exceptions.
▲ Give positive feedback more often than criticism.	▲ Be condescending.
▲ Hold staff accountable for implementing changes based on PD.	▲ Create blanket policies to address problems caused by a minority of staff members.
▲ Hold staff and yourself accountable for professional interactions and behavior.	▲ Avoid having difficult conversations with ineffective staff.
▲ Provide good food and coffee at staff and PD meetings.	▲ Usurp PD or PLC time for other purposes.
▲ Assume that teaches are doing their best. Trust that they are working their hardest.	▲ Have too many focuses for PD.
▲ Follow through—if you say you will do something, then do it. Be consistent.	▲ Change PD focus every year.
▲ Be approachable. Laugh, tell jokes, or have fun with staff. Poke fun at yourself.	▲ Undermine or throw staff under the bus with kids or parents.
▲ Communicate what you did with a kid who was sent to the office and why. Communicate it the same day.	▲ Spend time in staff meetings on subjects that could have been communicated through email.
▲ Socialize with staff—host a BBQ, ice cream social, luncheon, picnic.	▲ Spend time in staff meetings on proving that problems exist, instead of on finding solutions to those problems.

Listen to Teachers

The best place to start with a reluctant staff is to listen. Try to understand where their resistance comes from. Acknowledge it, rather than dismissing it, even when you feel that their upset is personally directed at you or is completely unfounded or unrealistic. An effective principal knows that their teachers have more direct knowledge about teaching and learning at the school than they do. Dr. Stephen Covey is famously quoted as saying that an effective leader "seeks to understand, before seeking to be understood." This is good advice for principals. Seek to hear what teachers perceive to be the biggest obstacles to learning, positive culture, change, and job satisfaction. Take what they have to say seriously, but not personally.

Bright Idea

Ask for staff feedback routinely; always give feedback in the way you would want to hear it.

RECOMMENDATION: Ask for staff feedback routinely, both formally and informally, throughout the year. Request that feedback always be "constructive and kind." Constructive means that people feel welcome to describe any problem and, if possible, propose a solution or a next step to explore. Kind means to share these details with some concern for how they will be received. A good rule of thumb is to always give feedback in the way you would want to hear it, if someone else was giving it to you. Model this for staff by giving them feedback routinely, both formally and informally, in a way that is constructive and kind. This will set the tone and encourage them to reciprocate.

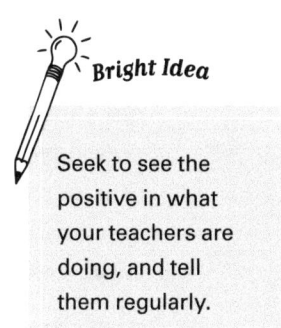

Bright Idea

Seek to see the positive in what your teachers are doing, and tell them regularly.

Let the Data Lead, Briefly

Lead with data, but don't get stuck on it. Data can be a powerful motivator; it helps schools to make strategic decisions about what resources they need and what they should invest in to address those needs. On the other hand, no teacher wants to sit in a staff meeting and disaggregate data for an hour, only to find that it tells them what they already knew — referrals are too high, or not enough kids are proficient in reading or math.

RECOMMENDATION: Avoid sharing raw data. The admin team can disaggregate the data and present a concise, 10-minute summary to staff, complete with their conclusions. The raw data can be made available to anyone interested in looking at it on their own time. In this way, the bulk of the time staff spends together can be spent on addressing the problems the data illuminates, brainstorming possible solutions, and planning for change.

Give Positive Feedback

Nobody wants to hear continual, difficult feedback, no matter how constructive. When negative feedback is given more often than positive feedback, the overall climate becomes one of critical evaluation.

RECOMMENDATION: Do regular classroom drop-ins. Stay five to ten minutes. Look at what students are doing. Before you leave the room, leave a sticky note on the teacher's desk. Or later that day, drop a note in the teacher's box. In the note, just say thank you and note at least one thing you liked, appreciated, or were impressed by. Also, for every critical piece of feedback or tough conversation you need to have with a teacher, strive for three or more genuine, positive interactions, no matter how small. Likewise, for every difficult truth you need to share with the entire staff at a staff meeting, share three things to celebrate.

Take Responsibility

No matter what role you play in your school, if you are not getting what you need and want from students when you interact with them, then first point the finger of responsibility at yourself. If you are the principal, and your staff is not behaving in the way you want, then do the same. Appropriate behavior and good decision-making are learned skills, just like reading or writing or any other traditional academic skill. Students can learn to act appropriately. It's the school's job to find a way to help them to do that. Teachers can learn to experiment with new techniques and work effectively together to produce change. It's the principal's job to find a way to help them.

> *"We change other people's behavior*
> *by changing our own."*
>
> — ANONYMOUS

From Grace

I remember once hearing a story in professional development about the famous behaviorist, BF Skinner. Skinner used to do experiments with pigeons, where he would put a pigeon in a box and then predict how it would behave when exposed to different stimuli. If the pigeon did not behave as expected, then he concluded that it was his fault, not the pigeon's. He started all his experiments with the underlying thesis that "the pigeon is always right."

If the work taking place in your school has not achieved the results you want, then the blame goes to every adult. Students need everyone to be working for their success. Administrators can't blame the teachers. Teachers can't blame one another, the administration, the students, or the community. When the data reveals a problem, then the principal must help teachers to confront the data—and their peers, if necessary. Kids are the ones to suffer when adults avoid talking about uncomfortable truths around ineffective teaching or discipline practices. It's understandable that as adults we want to protect egos and avoid confrontations—but these behaviors end up hurting kids. And none of us is here to hurt kids.

Office Referrals

In Chapter 4 we spoke at some length about the office referral process and the potential it has to help or hinder behavioral learning and build or destroy school culture. We will both revisit some of that information here and expand upon the specific role of administrators in forming and applying the referral process for the greatest good.

Straight Talk

Kids are the ones to suffer when adults avoid talking about uncomfortable truths around ineffective teaching.

The referral process is a constant, precarious issue for schools. When expectations are unclear or not being followed consistently, we end up with teachers losing their cool and sending a kid to the office for not having a pencil. Or the principal sends a Tier 3 student back to class much too quickly after the student created a major disruption in class. In these situations, both sides suffer and, more importantly, the student loses. Without adult clarity and consistency, struggling students cannot be successful. This is especially true for Tier 3 students, who often are veterans of constantly shifting expectations, reactions, and social structures.

Effective schools have created clear and regular communication between staff and administration about what happens when students are sent to the office and why. An agreement among all parties must be in place that defines what qualifies as an infraction, what will be done about it, and by whom. What should a teacher be expected to handle and in what manner? What is an administrator's role when an infraction calls for their direct intervention? Once these decisions are made, everyone needs to consistently follow the agreed-upon plan.

"Three With Me" Versus "One And Done"

One way to start a schoolwide effort to create clear disciplinary structures that can be consistently followed is to first get clarity about which behaviors are considered things that teachers should try to handle, control, or de-escalate in class and which behaviors warrant a referral out of the room for administrative consequences or intervention. This can be accomplished with a staff discussion on "one-and-done" infractions versus "three-with-me" infractions.

Any behavior—even if quite mild, if it becomes chronic or disruptive enough—can ultimately result in a student's being sent out. On the other hand, very few behaviors warrant being sent out without first trying to successfully redirect the student or de-escalate the situation first. Consider which behaviors and actions should immediately result in the student's leaving the room (one and done), and with which behaviors and actions the teacher should make at least three reasonable attempts, using three or more different consequences or techniques, to redirect the student before even considering sending out (three with me).

Listed below are some common examples that might be considered for each category:

Food for Thought

> Very few behaviors warrant a student's being sent out—without the teacher's trying to redirect them or de-escalate the situation first.

One and done

- ▲ Student throws heavy object at teacher or another student with intent to harm.

- ▲ Student physically attacks the teacher or another student.

- ▲ Student intentionally swears directly at the teacher.

- ▲ Student uses blatant homophobic, racist, or sexist language specifically for the purpose of intimidation.

Three with me

- ▲ Student throws object like paper or pencil with no intent to harm.
- ▲ Student yells at teacher or another student.
- ▲ Student swears.
- ▲ Student does not bring materials.
- ▲ Student uses inappropriate or belittling language.
- ▲ Student refuses to do work.
- ▲ Student is disruptive or distracting to others.
- ▲ Student is off-task.
- ▲ Student refuses to follow directions.

As a staff, create your own list. Role-play some scenarios. Practice using whisper discipline, soft eyes, and offering choices as detailed in Chapter 3. The more prepared you feel, and the more clarity you have, the easier this will be to implement — and the more successful the implementation will be.

The Referral Process

Once you have agreed as a staff on which infractions should be handled in the classroom and which should result in a referral to an administrator, the next step is to agree on a clear system of what happens next. What will the administration do when different students, with different behavior histories, are sent to the office for a variety of reasons? Start with things that will always happen, such as, "No student who is sent to the office will be sent back to class without talking to an adult." Or, "Students sent to the office will stay out of class for at least 10 minutes before being sent back to class." Or, "Students will not be sent back to class with a lollipop (literal or metaphorical) and an attitude of vindication." Decide as a staff what your deal-breakers are. After that, be clear about what each group wants. Discuss:

A Closer Look

Discuss as a staff how the referral policy can be improved to better meet everyone's needs—students, staff, and admin.

▲ What is the goal of sending a student to the office, from the point of view of an administrator and from that of a teacher?

▲ Are these goals compatible or incompatible? Are they realistic? Are they in the best interest of the student?

▲ What steps will administrative staff take with repeat offenders?

▲ How will administrative consequences be communicated to the referring teacher in a timely manner?

▲ Who will be responsible for communicating with parents?

It is essential that the staff feel heard about what they need from admin in order to feel supported when a student is sent out of class. It's equally important for administrators to be clear with teachers where they can meet the teacher's needs, where they can't, and why. Teachers feel unsupported and become resentful when they don't know whether infractions are being handled at all, or why infractions are being handled the way they are. Resentment leads to resistance and combative relationships, which is bad for everyone. Clarity and communication form the solution.

Don't Be Part of the Problem

It might also be necessary to lead a whole staff conversation about not being part of the problem. In struggling schools, a significant number of the behavioral infractions that end in referral or suspension are created by adults. This means that something an adult said or did made the situation worse, rather than better. This most often occurs when teachers are taking misbehavior personally and/or when they are no longer assuming the best about their students. Being up-front and explicit about the things all staff are no longer going to say and do when disciplining kids — and why — sets you up for discussing what you will do instead. You can pave the way for frank conversations of this nature by sharing research on how childhood trauma and toxic stress affect learning and behavior. (See Appendix E for research and resources). This can help you shift the negative assumptions that your more defensive or hostile teachers are likely harboring about their toughest students.

> ## From Scott
>
> During my first three months as a principal in a struggling, urban elementary school in the Midwest, some of the adult behaviors I witnessed were alarming. Some staff members were making poor choices in how they addressed kids, one another, and families. Their stress level was at a fever pitch, and it showed most significantly in how students were being talked to. In late October, a planned staff meeting was changed from the typical PD into one of adult conduct. By that time, I had amassed a list of events, quotes, and adult behaviors that were not okay, and that were not helping anyone to find success. We discussed these in an open forum, and then we banned certain language and actions—such as saying "shut up" to students or continuing to shout at students even after they have left the room. We also revised our handbook to reflect a commitment to professionalism in all aspects of our work.
>
> It was one of the best, but most uncomfortable, meetings I have ever been a part of. But it was so necessary to our progression, from the chaos of our past to the vision of our future. Lines and boundaries had to be addressed. And once they were, staff and administration alike made changes, slowly and with support, until adult-created discipline issues became a rarity.

Administrators can be part of the problem, too. We've discussed several ways administrators influence referrals and suspensions, in relation to specific situations. The three most relevant for principals are:

1. Not having an effective process for what to do with kids once they are sent to the office.

Straight Talk

In struggling schools, a significant number of the behavioral infractions that end in referral or suspension are created by adults.

2. Not communicating clearly to teachers what happened, and why, after kids were sent to the office.

3. Making policies that undercut teachers like, "Don't send kids to the office on a referral unless they are a danger to self or others."

From Scott

A colleague of mine was the principal at an elementary school that frequently experienced high behavioral referral days. One day, out of sheer frustration, the principal announced, via the intercom, that there were to be no more referrals to the office for the remainder of the day. The students then knew that consequences were no longer on the table for them. As you can imagine, total chaos ensued.

All schools should make strategic plans to lower their referral and suspension rates, especially if their referral rate is above district and state averages. High referral and suspension rates are generally indicators of two problems occurring on a campus: lack of teacher training around de-escalation and appropriate discipline structures; and lack of schoolwide intervention resources and personnel. Making a "no referrals" policy to lower referral and suspension rates, however, is akin to treating the symptom of a disease, instead of the cause. High referral and suspension rates are the result of the problem, not the cause. Policies of this kind undermine the ability of teachers to enforce clear behavioral expectations and boundaries with their most challenging kids. See more on this in Chapter 4.

Straight Talk

Making a "no referrals" policy to lower referral and suspension rates is akin to treating the symptom of a disease, instead of the cause.

The Four-Week Experimentation Cycle

The four-week experimentation cycle, sometimes called the "four-week cycle of change," is a simple way to help staff make small, realistic changes in a supportive environment. Before beginning a cycle, two scaffolds must be in place to ensure the cycle's success.

First, get on the same page. Look at your behavioral data, referrals, suspensions, and expulsions and determine what they are telling you. Then evaluate your current classroom and schoolwide discipline systems. What's working? What's not? Where do changes need to occur? Have conversations, such as the ones proposed earlier in this chapter, about who should be handling what and how.

Bright Idea

Share 10 techniques you see teachers using to effectively support their toughest kids. Ask everyone on staff to experiment for one week with one technique that is new to them.

Second, provide some discipline training and new resources. Chapter 3 in this book is a good place to start. Other things you might consider are: intervention strategies from Chapter 5; a structured study on a discipline-based book, such as Conscious Classroom Management, 2nd Edition, by Rick Smith and Grace Dearborn; inviting an expert to do a workshop on discipline techniques with the staff; or sharing 10 things that you see teachers on campus doing that seem to be working with tough kids. Whatever you choose to bring in or share, make sure it involves practical strategies that teachers can immediately experiment with in their classes.

Once you have discussed what needs to change, supported your conclusions with data, and exposed the staff to practical techniques that might bring about these changes, you are ready to try an experimentation cycle. Staff meetings, PLC meetings, PD meetings, or any other regular weekly meeting time can be used for this purpose. Here's how:

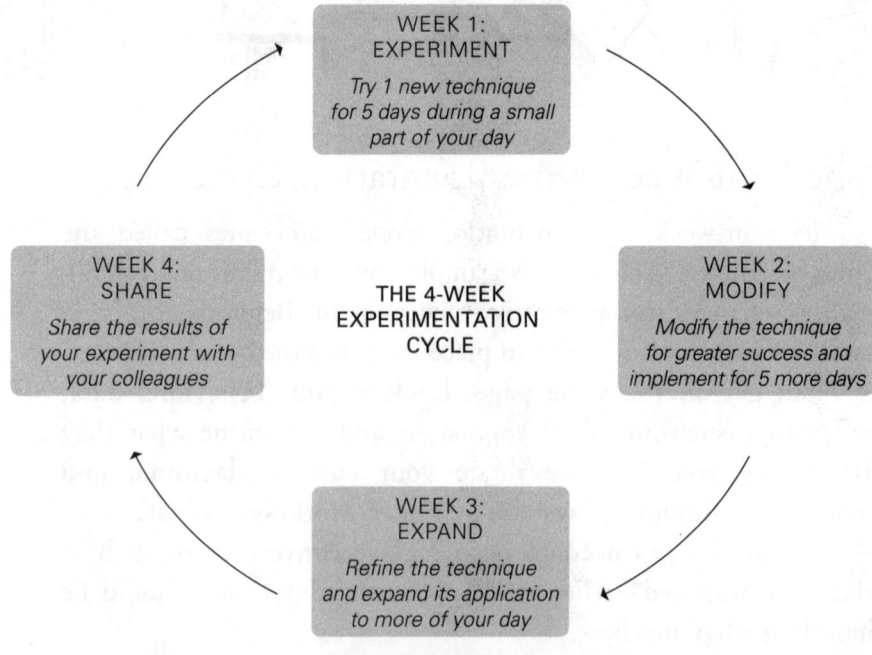

Week 1: Experiment

At a staff meeting, propose an experiment to your staff. Ask teachers to choose any new idea, strategy, or technique that interests them from Chapter 3 in this book—and try it for one hour a day, for one week in their classrooms. Set them up for success by initially encouraging them to choose the easiest hour of their day, when they and their students tend to be at their best. Alternately, they can try a new technique with just one or two specific students for one week. Once teachers have selected what they will try, have them group together with other teachers who chose the same technique or student(s). You can further separate groups by grade level or department. Schedule time when these small groups can discuss how, when, and with whom they will try the new plan and commit to trying it for five school days.

For example, in an elementary school, one group of teachers decides they want to try using the language of offering choices before giving out consequences. They agree to try this during the last 90 minutes of the day for one week.

In a secondary school, one group of teachers decides that they want to try soft eyes and whisper discipline with a specific student that they share. They agree to each try it with that student for five school days.

During the five days, each teacher tries their chosen strategy, making modifications and adjustments as needed to make it work with their student(s) and to counter any resistance. Teachers also note their own resistance to the change and reflect on the simplest steps they can take to counter that resistance.

Week 2: Modify

At a staff meeting, teachers meet in their small groups to discuss their experiences with the first week of implementation. They share successes, challenges, and modifications. Ask them to commit to another week of implementation, making use of suggestions from their group for modification. Encourage teachers to set up peer observations, to watch each other as they attempt this second week of implementation. Or encourage them to video themselves for 15 minutes and then share the video with a trusted colleague for feedback.

Week 3: Expand

At a staff meeting, teachers meet in their small groups to discuss their findings from the second week of implementation. If any peer observations occurred, or if video was shot, these can be shared and discussed here. Teachers compare and contrast the effectiveness of the strategy from the first week of implementation to the second. Teachers decide on any final modifications they will make for the third week of implementation and decide how they will expand their use of the strategy to more students or to more parts of their days.

Week 4: Share

At staff meeting, teachers share with the whole staff what they tried over the last three weeks and how it went. They explain what they plan to keep — and share — and what they plan to discard, and why. For the next week, teachers integrate what they've already begun and start to consider what technique they will try for the next experimentation cycle.

Repeat the Cycle

The following week, the cycle begins again, with new groups and new strategies to implement. All groups try another, different technique from Chapter 3. Although you might have some groups who would like to select techniques from Chapter 5 on one-on-one interventions, we highly recommend that all staff first try at least two experimentation cycles with two different techniques from Chapter 3. This is the place where we take proactive steps to intervene more appropriately with difficult students. This helps to ensure that we are not over-identifying Tier 3 kids.

Bright Idea

Encourage your teachers to record themselves for 15 minutes and then share the video with a trusted colleague.

Create Accountability

Identifying the school's toughest issues and finding the resources, trainings, and materials necessary to address those issues is the easy part. The hard part is actually getting an entire staff to try something new, and to stick with it for an extended period of time. The four-week experimentation cycle will help, but you also need to create some accountability around trying.

Bright Idea

Be explicit with your staff that you would rather see them try new things and fail, than not try at all.

Start by being explicit: You would rather see teachers try new things and fail, than not try at all. If we keep doing what we are doing, we will keep getting what we are getting. As a staff, if we have decided that what we are getting isn't good enough, then everyone has to experiment with doing things differently. The kids are not going to change unless we change first. However, if the staff feel that you're only looking for quick success — and that the new program and training don't allow for well-intentioned attempts that might ultimately fail — then many won't even try.

No matter what you do or say, some teachers will still resist trying new things, both passively and aggressively. Teachers who refuse to try, or who say they tried but can't show any evidence that they did, need one-on-one help to move them past their resistance. If they are never confronted about their resistance, and never experience an uncomfortable individual consequence for that resistance, then they will simply do nothing. Check out Todd Whitaker's book, *Dealing with Difficult Teachers*, or Jen Abram's *Having Hard Conversations* if you need some help preparing for accountability conversations with resistant teachers.

Be careful, however, that you don't institute policies meant to rein in your most reactive or resistant teachers, instead of working with those teachers one-on-one. As mentioned earlier, this is often how schools end up with blanket "no referrals" policies that effectively hamstring proactive teachers, removing a consequence they need at their disposal.

As site leaders, we need to be willing to intervene with and support our reactive and resistant teachers individually, no matter how uncomfortable it makes us or them. Policies should be written to meet the needs of our most effective teachers. When teachers abuse, misuse, or misinterpret the policy, you take them aside for individual help. It's no different from running an effective classroom. You don't punish an

Food for Thought

Change is uncomfortable. But if we aren't uncomfortable, then we aren't growing.

entire class because four kids can't follow the rules. You don't lower your academic expectations for an entire unit because four kids are functionally illiterate. You teach rigorous lessons, work with those four kids individually—modifying, scaffolding, accommodating, and differentiating as necessary—while simultaneously appreciating the rest if the class for doing the right thing. Likewise, you don't make policies that cripple all your teachers because four teachers are abusing or misusing the policy.

Review and Reflect

As part of an ongoing review, staff and administration should repeatedly evaluate all infractions, as well as the manner in which they are handled. Patterns, data, and inconsistencies must be placed out in the open and discussed, so that productive changes can be made. These discussions can be uncomfortable and awkward, especially when an inconsistent teacher or administrator is forced to face their missteps. When handled well, however, these discussions are critical to establishing trust, making changes, and building consistency. In the end, if we aren't uncomfortable, then we aren't growing.

It's up to the administrator to set a tone of inclusivity and to model respectful communication for these discussions. All voices must be heard for these discussions to achieve long-term, positive results. That means that administrators need to be open to discussing where they have strayed from the system and what they plan to do to improve their consistency. If a school as a whole is going to effect change, then the staff must clearly see that the administration is not above reflecting, changing, and taking responsibility for their own failures, big and small.

Patience and Pressure

Successfully leading change grows from the proper combination of patience and pressure. The system within the school is the basis of the pressure. The principal is the vehicle of the pressure, providing the road map that guides the school to positive behavioral outcomes. The task is daunting for everyone involved, administrators, teachers, and students. Patience greases the wheels. To deal with the pressure, and with one another, everyone needs patience with the process. Usually, multiple years are required to achieve noticeable success. In our experience, it takes at least three years to create a sustainable system.

Food for Thought

Creating change in behavioral systems, techniques, and attitudes is a marathon, not a sprint.

Creating sustainable change is much more difficult than it sounds, as anyone who has tried to do it will testify. One might think that once a new system is rolled out—and you've even seen some small, positive results—this system would gain momentum. One might think that such a functional system would take on a life of its own, and even become self-sustaining. One would be wrong. As when planting a new flowering shrub in the garden, initially the shrub is fragile. Even if it produces new growth and flowers during the first season, it might be killed or damaged by frost, insects, mold, poor soil, inadequate drainage, or a dozen other things, especially while it's young and newly transplanted. In schools, when new systems are put in place, initial successes are small and hard-won. Teachers can burn out on the effort. Resilience declines after the first few months, and even normal and predictable setbacks can lead teachers to revert to older, more familiar ways.

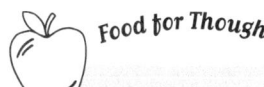

Food for Thought

The key to maintaining enthusiasm and longevity with a new system is to set small, realistic goals, celebrate successes frequently, maintain consistent but mild pressure, and, above all, be patient.

Creating change in behavioral systems, techniques, and attitudes is, as they say, a marathon, not a sprint. We have to be in it for the long haul. The school didn't become dysfunctional overnight, and it certainly will not change overnight. Setbacks will occur. That doesn't mean the system isn't working. The system is also merely a plan; it's not carved in stone. It will need to be adjusted over time to fit the realities of the school. An identified area of need might quickly vanish, and a new area might arise. The plan must be flexible enough to deal with such changes.

The key to maintaining enthusiasm and longevity with a new system is to set small, realistic goals, celebrate successes frequently, add supports as necessary, maintain consistent but mild pressure, and, above all, be patient. The adults must understand and agree to the plan and then practice patience. We need the kind of patience we exhibit when teaching a child to ride a bike. Failure, scrapes, crying, and frustration are expected! So, too, goes the world of building success within classroom and schoolwide behavioral systems. If everyone says out loud, "We will make mistakes, we will become frustrated, we will disappoint ourselves and one another, but that's okay," then it will be okay. Hope is being open to the possibility; faith is a belief that it will happen. Start with hope, search for faith, and we will all reach the promised land together.

▲ ▲ ▲

Yeah Buts & What Ifs…

Administrator: What if some of my staff get upset when I point out or celebrate their colleagues' successes?

Celebrating success is essential. If this practice is not already the norm at the school, then you've just found your first task. If celebrating success makes some people feel uncomfortable, that's okay. Acknowledge the discomfort. "We are a team. When one member of our team hits a home run, we all get to celebrate. Some people are going to hit more home runs than others. But we cannot ignore the batter who hit a home run because another player struck out. We also will be celebrating more than just home runs. We will celebrate catching fly balls and stealing bases. We won't limit ourselves to celebrating successes, either, and also will celebrate effort and experimentation, even when those efforts fail.

We are in this together." This job is way too hard to be ignoring effort and successes just to avoid upset feelings. So celebrate with your staff every chance you get. If you have a few staff members who are particularly resistant or struggling, look especially hard for something to celebrate them for.

Administrator: What if a few of my teachers dig in and refuse to attempt any change?

If what you are doing fits within the expectations of the district, then you can use the district's formal or informal processes with resistant staff members. Start by assuming the best; hold the thought that if they knew better, they would do better. Meet with them. Listen to what they have to say about why they are not on board, why they are not trying new things. Then, with kindness, increase the pressure and decrease the patience. Be clear with them about what needs to happen. Set "experimentation," not success, as the goal. Be clear that you would rather see them try something new and fail than not try at all. State the need for this experimentation from the perspective of what their students need, not what you need.

Be specific and concrete about what strategy or techniques you want them to try and within what time frame you want them to experiment. Offer to help. Explain what resources or support you can offer. Then schedule a follow-up meeting for two weeks out to discuss progress and results. Let them know the different possibilities for that meeting—depending on whether they do, or don't, make an attempt to meet your stated expectation. In the interim, drop by their classroom. Have a couple of informal conversations during the first week to see what's happening so far. If they are passively resisting, then tighten the screws. Send a mentor or instructional coach to work with them on getting started. Having hard conversations, sharing the difficult truth, and

Straight Talk

Having hard conversations and placing pressure on reluctant staff is incredibly uncomfortable, but in some cases it's the only way to create change.

placing pressure on reluctant staff is incredibly uncomfortable, but in some cases it's the only way to create change. Sooner is better than later. Students can't wait for you to get comfortable with being in charge, and they can't wait for their teachers to have personal epiphanies before being willing to change.

> **Administrator: Won't sharing my own concerns, and admitting to my own mistakes, make me look weak?**

Hiding from the truth is the only weakness. Staff will see and feel any mistakes you make. Pretending that they don't exist will only make you look incompetent and insecure. Schools need strong, positive leaders who can motivate a staff toward a common goal. Teachers admire honesty and a willingness to be vulnerable in their principal. Most of all, they admire a leader who walks the talk. Strength as a leader does not come from never being wrong. It comes from taking responsibility, making necessary changes, connecting with staff members, modeling the qualities and effort you want from your staff, creating gentle but firm accountability, and making decisions that are in everyone's best interest.

▲ ▲ ▲

Summary & Applications

Remember

▲ Change is possible, but also hard. Be patient. Results are slow to manifest. Stay the course.

▲ Lead by example. Get uncomfortable. Be vulnerable, listen to staff, and be open to making your own changes.

▲ Give staff three pieces of positive feedback for every one difficult piece of feedback.

▲ Give difficult feedback in a kind and constructive way, and encourage staff to do the same.

▲ Staff meetings, PD time, or PLCs can be used for ongoing reflection and discussion groups focused on experimenting with new behavioral techniques in the classroom.

Discuss

▲ Does your school have high teacher turn-over? If so, what factors contribute most to this? Are you one of the factors? Where are the opportunities for you to grow and change, or for you to change systems and policies, to lower teacher turn-over?

▲ What resistance do you feel to surveying your staff about your effectiveness as a leader? How might you overcome this resistance?

▲ How often do you give positive feedback to staff as a group and to individual teachers personally? How often to do you give critical feedback? How can you easily increase the frequency of your positive feedback without creating an unmanageable time-suck?

▲ Reflect on several difficult conversations you have had with staff members, especially ones that did not go well or that you wish you had handled differently. If you could go back in time, how could you have communicated necessary feedback in a more kind and constructive way, without being either a pushover or a bully?

▲ How do you use your staff meeting time? Can any of the information you give during this time be condensed or communicated by email instead? What other ways could you free up time for staff to plan together, or share successes, regarding implementation of new ideas and behavioral techniques?

▲ What staff resistance can you expect or anticipate as you try to roll out new behavioral systems, techniques, or expectations? How can you meet this resistance in a productive way and help move your teachers past it?

Apply

▲ Give the "Dos and Don'ts of Effective Leadership" found on page 183 to your staff. Have them anonymously highlight which things they think describe you in each column. Review their feedback. Choose one thing that several (or a majority of) staff highlighted in the "DON'T" column and one thing that several (or a majority of) staff did NOT highlight in the "DO" column. Make a plan to alter your leadership style to address these.

▲ Have a "three-with-me versus one-and-done" discussion with staff about office referrals. Find consensus. Create clarity. Revise your policy as necessary.

▲ Meet with teachers individually if they are overusing referrals. Together, look at their last month's referrals; look for patterns and trends, and discuss alternatives.

▲ Have a frank conversation with staff about words and actions that need to simply stop. Give them a written list. Ask them if there are other things they want to add to the list. Be open to the possibility that they will add things that you say and do, things they want you to stop.

▲ Ask for staff feedback regularly, both formally and informally. Take what staff says seriously and plan to make changes where possible.

▲ Practice how you will kindly confront individual teachers who need more pressure to attempt proactive changes. Do this in a firm but caring way. Role-play what you might say and do during this conversation. Have a trusted friend or family member play the resistant teacher.

▲ Provide staff with practical training and support resources around de-escalating volatile behaviors and intervening with off-task behaviors. Then run a four-week experimentation cycle with staff.

7

A PLAN
FOR CHANGE

> *"We do well when we all do well."*
>
> — ELEANOR ROOSEVELT,
> FIRST LADY AND SOCIAL ACTIVIST

I N CHAPTER 1, WE TALKED ABOUT WHO TIER 3 KIDS ARE, how they differ from Tier 2 kids, and why understanding the distinction is important.

In Chapter 2, we talked about how our beliefs aid or hinder our ability to work effectively with Tier 3 kids, and we looked at one specific technique — the Invisible Subtitle — that can help any educator to develop productive beliefs about difficult kids.

In Chapter 3, we looked at the specifics of classroom-based discipline and intervention, including how and why to build flexible hierarchies of consequences — and how to address basic resistance or misbehavior in a way that strengthens relationships, teaches behavioral lessons, and keeps everyone on the same side. We also looked at how to de-escalate confrontations with oppositional kids, and the specific verbal and nonverbal techniques you can use to accomplish this.

In Chapter 4, we discussed schoolwide discipline and interventions, including the different, concrete pieces of these that you can adopt or adapt to better meet the needs of Tier 3 kids when they are sent out of the classroom.

In Chapter 5, we looked at how to put together formal and informal one-on-one interventions with Tier 3 students who need more than excellent teaching and effective schoolwide supports in order to be successful.

In Chapter 6, we focused on how to effectively lead a school and staff through making changes. Principals were shown how to inspire staff to work together to create or revise discipline and intervention systems, how to encourage staff buy-in around trying new things, and how to lead by example — through making personal changes, being vulnerable, taking responsibility, and giving feedback in kind and constructive ways.

Here, in our final chapter, we provide a sample timeline and template for how to incorporate all of these things into a three-year plan for overall school improvement.

▲ ▲ ▲

Suggested Three-Year Plan

As you look through this suggested plan, consider which elements you might adopt or adapt. This plan is not meant to be used as-is, but rather as a starting place to consider how you might create or modify your own plan. Moreover, this plan only focuses on making behavior-related changes—changes to classroom and schoolwide discipline systems and interventions. It does not include the dozens of other things a school would simultaneously be working on, such as academic instruction and other school or district initiatives. Finally, this plan is for administrators who have been at their school sites for more than one year. If this is your first year at a school, we suggest you use the next several months to watch, listen, assess, and build relationships. These are necessary first steps in understanding the issues at the school. Use your first year to recruit a leadership team, survey staff about what changes they want to see, and start laying the groundwork to begin a three-year, schoolwide implementation during your second year.

Year 1: Assess, Plan, Expose, Experiment

1ˢᵗ Quarter	**Take Stock:**
	▲ Survey staff, parents, and students.
	▲ What are the school's shortcomings, needs, and strengths?
	▲ What is working well to address student behavior and school culture, and what is not? How do we know?
	• Review behavioral data for the last 3 to 5 years. Look for trends and areas of high need.
	• Inventory existing, available resources for classroom and schoolwide behavior management.
	Share with Staff:
	▲ Share survey results and past behavioral data. Discuss what can be concluded from these pieces of evidence about what is going well and what needs to be addressed.
	▲ Share a rough outline of your three-year plan to improve behavior, climate, and culture. Get feedback from staff. Be open to modifications.

1st Quarter *Continued*	**Plan with Staff:** ▲ Set Year 1 expectations and objectives. ▲ Recruit a Leadership Team.
2nd Quarter	**Begin a Book Study:** ▲ Use this book or another book that provides practical behavioral techniques that teachers can select and try immediately, such as *Conscious Classroom Management*, 2nd Edition, by Rick Smith and Grace Dearborn. **Revise Referral System:** ▲ Review trends in 1st quarter referrals and suspensions. ▲ Discuss common situations that end in referral. Brainstorm alternative classroom techniques and teacher modifications that can reduce referrals and better meet student needs. ▲ Have a "three-with-me versus one-and-done" discussion. Come to consensus. ▲ Get feedback from teachers about changes they'd like to see in both the system as a whole and how it's implemented. Be honest about what you can and cannot do to accommodate their wishes. ▲ Determine how referrals will be handled, tracked, and communicated to teachers. **Do Informal Observations:** ▲ Do as many as possible. ▲ Leave thank-you notes for observed teachers, stating one thing you appreciated or liked about what you saw or heard. Do not leave any critical feedback. ▲ Collect evidence of things to celebrate and look for overarching needs and widespread issues to be addressed with the entire staff.
3rd Quarter	**Continue Book Study.** **Experiment with New Techniques:** ▲ Put teachers in teams or allow them to choose their own teams. Have each team choose and try a new technique from the book study or any previous training, using the four-week experimentation cycle (Chapter 6). **Review 2nd-quarter Behavioral Data:** ▲ Celebrate any success, no matter how small. ▲ Look for trends to address.

3rd Quarter *Continued*	▲ Discuss what's working so far and what isn't. Brainstorm solutions and modifications.
	▲ Begin informally checking in with teachers who send the most referrals or seem the most reluctant to change.
	Research Resources for Year 2:
	▲ With your leadership team, start looking into resources, trainings, and personnel that you might want to include next year. Use them to continue supporting the schoolwide behavioral, socio-emotional, and cultural goals.
	▲ Start figuring out where to find the money to pay for these extra resources, and how to schedule them into next year's calendar.
	Continue Informal Observations.
4th Quarter	**Finish Book Study.**
	Continue Experimenting with New Techniques:
	▲ Put teachers in new teams, allow them to choose new teams, or allow them to continue with previous teams. Have each team choose and try a new technique from the book study or any previous training, using the four week experimentation cycle.
	Review 3rd-quarter Behavioral Data:
	▲ Celebrate any success, no matter how small.
	▲ Look for ongoing trends and new issues to address.
	▲ Discuss what's working so far and what isn't. Brainstorm solutions and modifications.
	▲ Continue to informally check in with teachers who write the most referrals or are resisting schoolwide changes.
	Plan for Year 2:
	▲ Schedule trainings and acquire resources for next year's PD.
	▲ Give an end-of-year survey to staff.
	▲ Look at 4th-quarter behavioral data.
	▲ Start formulating expectations and goals for next year.
	▲ Prioritize creating and staffing an ISI Room, or some behavior-intervention equivalent.
	▲ Celebrate successes.

Year 2: Schoolwide Implementation

1ˢᵗ Quarter	**Take Stock:**
	▲ Review behavioral data and teacher surveys from last year, compare and contrast to the previous year. Summarize findings.
	Share with Staff:
	▲ Share behavioral data and staff survey summary with staff. Celebrate any Year 1 successes. Address any big concerns.
	▲ Revisit vision and three-year plan. Set Year 2 goals and objectives.
	Communicate Any New Expectations/Routines:
	▲ Review how the office-referral system will be different /improved.
	▲ Introduce the ISI Room and explain how it will work (Chapter 4).
	Plan Inspirational/Practical Keynote on Behavior:
	▲ Make sure to offer at least a half-dozen simple, discrete techniques that teachers can try right away.
2ⁿᵈ Quarter	**Begin a Book Study:**
	▲ Choose a book that provides practical behavioral techniques that teachers can select and try immediately.
	Experiment with New Classroom Techniques:
	▲ Put teachers in teams or allow them to choose their own teams. Have each team choose and try a new technique from last year's book study or this year's keynote or PD training, using the four-week experimentation cycle.
	Look at 1st-quarter Behavioral Ddata:
	▲ Celebrate any success, no matter how small.
	▲ Look for trends to address.
	▲ Discuss what's working so far and what isn't.
	▲ Make modifications to create greater success.
	Meet with Resistant Teachers:
	▲ Increase pressure on them to experiment with new techniques.

"Coming together is a beginning; keeping together is progress; working together is success."

—HENRY FORD, BUSINESSMAN & ENTREPRENEUR

2nd Quarter *Continued*	▲ Brainstorm and provide support for them around challenging kids and situations. ▲ Attach some form of accountability and consequence for continuing to be uncooperative. **Start Informal Observations.**
3rd Quarter	**Continue Book Study.** **Continue 4-Week Experimentation Cycles.** **Look at 2nd-quarter Behavioral Data. Celebrate Successes, Discuss Necessary Modifications:** ▲ Celebrate successes, discuss necessary modifications. **Research Resources for Next Year.** **Continue Informal Observations.** **Continue to Meet with Resistant Teachers.**
4th Quarter	**Finish Book Study.** **Have Small Teams Continue to Experiment with New Classroom Techniques in Four Week Cycles.** **Review 3rd-quarter Behavioral Data. Celebrate Successes, Discuss Necessary Modifications.** **Plan for Year 3:** ▲ Schedule trainings and acquire resources for next year's PD. ▲ Give an end-of-year survey to staff. ▲ Look at 4th-quarter behavioral data. ▲ Start formulating expectations and goals for next year. ▲ Prioritize having teachers do peer observations, video-record themselves, reflect on their teaching, and start swaddle interventions with a few Tier 3 kids.

Year 3: Deepen Schoolwide Implementation

1ˢᵗ Quarter	**Take Stock:**
	▲ Review behavioral data and teacher surveys from last year, compare and contrast to the previous two years. Summarize findings.
	Share with Staff:
	▲ Share behavioral data and staff survey summary with staff. Celebrate any Year 2 successes. Address big concerns.
	▲ Revisit vision and three-year plan. Set Year 3 goals and objectives.
	Communicate Any New Expectations/Routines:
	▲ Review how the office-referral system will be different / improved.
	▲ Review how ISI Room will be changed/improved.
	▲ Introduce the idea of peer observations and videoing lessons for reflection (Chapter 6).
	▲ Introduce swaddle interventions for Tier 3 kids who need it, along with the use of Trusted Adults (Chapter 5).
	▲ Start collecting volunteers to make inroads in each of these areas.
	Plan Inspirational/Practical Keynote on Behavior:
	▲ Make sure to offer at least a half-dozen simple, discrete techniques that teachers can try right away.
2ⁿᵈ Quarter	**Begin a Book Study:**
	▲ Choose a book that provides practical behavioral techniques that teachers can select and try immediately.
	Experiment with Peer Observations & Video:
	▲ As teacher teams experiment with new techniques on the four-week cycle, have them video-record themselves or have a trusted peer observe them so they can reflect together. Plan to make substitutes available to cover peer observations.
	Look at 1st-quarter Behavioral Data:
	▲ Celebrate any successes, discuss positive and negative trends, make plans to modify as necessary.

2nd Quarter *Continued*	**Meet with Resistant Teachers.** **Do Informal Observations.**
3rd Quarter	**Continue Book Study.** **Continue Experimenting with New Techniques.** **Continue Peer Observations and Videoing.** **Look at 2nd-quarter Behavioral Data:** ▲ Celebrate successes, discuss necessary modifications. **Research Resources for Next Year.** **Continue Informal Observations.** **Meet with Resistant Teachers.**
4th Quarter	**Finish Book Study.** **Continue Experimenting with New Techniques.** **Continue Experimenting with Peer Observations & Video.** **Review 3rd-quarter Behavioral Data:** ▲ Celebrate successes, discuss necessary modifications. **Plan for Next Year:** ▲ Schedule trainings and acquire resources for next year's PD. ▲ Give an end-of-year survey to staff. ▲ Look at 4th-quarter behavioral data. ▲ Start formulating expectations and goals for next year.

From Scott

My last school was, and still is, a high-poverty, minority-majority school in the inner city of the largest urban district in the state. The school had had no formal, schoolwide behavior-management plan for many years prior to my arrival.

Although behavior had always been an issue, very little data had been kept on student behaviors. Therefore, we re-created a rough Year 1 baseline of behavior data, and found that over 22% of the students had been suspended at least once, and referrals were in the 2000+ range—for a total student body of 450 students, pre-K to 6th grade. Before the end of Year 1, schoolwide discipline planning was established. Plans were put in place for external supports through consultation. Internal systems of expectations, procedures, and routines were created. Then, for the next three years, suspensions and referrals steadily dropped, resulting in a nearly-70% reduction overall. In addition, every measure of climate, for every group—students, staff, and parents—showed positive gains. We were collecting data on positive supports and all behavioral referrals, and we were meeting regularly to assess our progress. Quite simply, we changed the culture and climate of the school in regard to discipline. At the same time, we increased our academic achievement significantly, even earning local awards for those gains.

At the end of a three-year implementation of the kind outlined in this chapter, you will absolutely see improvement worth writing home about. Maybe even worth singing from the mountain tops. That improvement will not just show up in lower referral and suspension rates; it will also show up in teacher satisfaction and student test scores. When everyone is working together to better meet the needs of our most vulnerable and challenging students, teachers are less overwhelmed and students are more engaged. The rising tide of positive school culture and behavioral intervention lifts all ships, including the ship of academic success. As Eleanor Roosevelt said, "We do well, when we all do well." Let us go forth, and all do well.

APPENDICES

APPENDIX A

5 Rs Resources

Release — Emotionally purge negative feelings

Create an entry-and-"release" procedure for entering the ISI Room that is simple and posted on a large, clear poster. For example:

1. Put your referral/pass in basket.

2. Go to a designated "cool-down" spot.

3. Play/Interact with any objects at your spot:
   Hit, Mangle, Cuddle, Draw, Write.

4. Stay at your spot until an adult comes to get you.

Recover — Generate internal calm through a mindfulness practice

In a binder or on an electronic tablet or laptop, have a selection of "recovery" mindfulness practices that students can choose from. Create a space in the room with pillows or soft mats to sit on, and place a binder or tablet with headphones at each spot. Recovery activities might include:

▲ **4-7-8 Breathing:** Inhale through the nose for a count of 4, hold breath for count of 7, exhale with a whooshing sound out of the mouth for a count of 8. Repeat 4 or more times.

▲ **Body Scan:** With eyes closed, take a deep breath in, exhale slowly. Notice how each part of your body feels, starting with the toes and going all the way up to the top of the head. Guided body scans can be supported with audio and written scripts. Find 3 to start with at www.consciousteaching.com/thiskid/resources.

▲ **Tense and Release:** Take a deep breath in through the nose, hold briefly, exhale. Repeat. Start by tensing your feet, hold for a few seconds, then exhale while releasing the feet. Notice the difference in your muscles between when they are tense and when they are relaxed. Move on to your legs and repeat by tensing, holding, and releasing with an exhale. Again notice the different feeling in your legs between tense and released states. Repeat with your butt, stomach, chest, hands, arms, shoulders, and face. A guided script can be found at www. consciousteaching.com/thiskid/resources.

▲ **Count the Colors:** Look around the room and name 6 things that are blue, then 5 things that are green, then 4 things that are yellow, then 3 things that are red, then 2 things that are orange. Note: Any 5 colors can be selected, and colors can be in any order. Or, look around the room and count how many things are blue. Then count how many things are green. How many things are yellow. How many things are red. And finally, how many things are orange.

▲ **The 5-4-3-2-1 Game:** Look around the room and silently name:
  • Five things in the room you can touch with your hands or feet.
  • Four things you can see in the room.
  • Three things you can hear in the room.
  • Two things you can smell in the room.
  • One good food you like to eat.

▲ **Yoga/Stretching:** Do 5 yoga poses. Hold still in each pose for 30 seconds or for 5 deep breaths before moving to the next pose. When done with all 5 poses, lay down in corpse pose and relax your entire body for a minute. Then repeat: Do all 5 poses again, exactly as before. Again, end with corpse pose. A selection of online yoga resources for teaching and/or guiding mindfulness yoga stretching with kids and teens can be found at www.consciousteaching.com/thiskid/resources

Reflect — Discuss and dissect what happened

Reflection begins with asking the student to describe the incident that brought them into the room. Additional prompts encourage the student to reflect on their thoughts and feelings before and during the incident. This will help them to begin to identify what event or feeling triggers their behavior. It is important to acknowledge any attempts the student made to cope with the problem in an appropriate way, even if the attempt failed. This will encourage them to try again in the future. Possible questions to guide the discussion:

▲ Please describe what happened.

▲ Who was involved?

▲ Where and when did it take place?

▲ Why do you think this happened?

▲ What thoughts did you have while this was happening?

▲ How did you feel when this was happening? Note: You might want to use a poster with feeling faces to help prompt younger children.

▲ What sensations did you notice in your body? Note: A laminated outline of a body — where younger children can write and to which teens can point — might help them describe the sensations they felt in their bodies.

▲ What did you need before or during the incident? Note: A list of potential needs might provide a helpful prompt. Some common needs are space, time, attention, help, food, rest, quiet, and/or understanding.

▲ How did your actions affect others? Note: A list of prompts might be helpful if the student is not able to think of things on their own. Such a list might include statements such as, "interrupted others' learning," "hurt others' feelings," "made environment unsafe," and/or "destroyed others' property."

- ▲ How did you try to solve the problem? If this is a repeat visit to ISI, add: What coping skills did you try since the last time you were here?

- ▲ What did you do that worked?

- ▲ What could you have done differently?

Reset — Set behavioral/emotional goals and practice coping mechanisms

Resetting comes directly on the heels of reflecting on what happened. In this portion of the process, we move away from the facts of what happened and into how to avoid having it happen again. You might start with questions, such as:

- ▲ How are you feeling now?

- ▲ What else do you need in order to be ready to return to class?

- ▲ What coping skills can you use if you get triggered again, after going back to class? Note: See options and resources below.

Have the student create a list of triggers that push their buttons. Or use a pre-created list, such as the one at https://www.teacherspayteachers. com/Product/What-Pushes-Your-Buttons-Anger-Triggers-2048633. Identify what trigger occurred with the current incident. Some actions that might trigger students include being told what to do, feeling left out, being touched, hearing loud noises, or receiving bad grades. Next, have the student describe what happens when their buttons are pushed. Refer back to today's incident, and make sure it's included on their list. Help the student to identify the early warning signs that precede an explosion — the sensations they feel and where in their body they feel them. Finally, have them list one or two things they could do next time they feel like they are heading for an explosion. The tools listed in the "Recover" section above are all useful as coping strategies: deep breathing, body scanning, tense and release, counting colors. Below are a few other options.

▲ **Positive self-talk:** Have the student create a list of 5 positive things they can say to themselves when they feel anxious or angry. The list can be written on paper or a note card and kept in their binder or desk, where they can refer to it whenever needed. They should practice the list daily, even if they are not having negative thoughts or anxiety.

▲ **Visualize a favorite or safe place:** Have the student close their eyes and visualize a favorite place. Have them describe it to you in detail, using all their senses. Time permitting, print out or have the student draw a version of this place on a note card or piece of paper. The next time they feel anxious, they can bring up this visualization for themselves, or look at the drawing/image. The student should practice this once a day at school, preferably during a time of day when they most often get triggered.

▲ **Taking space:** Have the student identify resources that help them to remove themselves from a challenging situation, when they feel like they can't control their feelings and might explode. For example, they can choose: a location, such as a rocking chair in back of the room; a person, such as a Trusted Adult; or an activity, such as getting a drink of water. Brainstorm how the student can nonverbally communicate to the teacher when their big feelings start to surface; perhaps a hand-signal can mean, "I need to leave my seat." Practice having the student use the hand signal and then walking to the back of the room or out into the hallway. Note: This technique will require a previous conversation with the teacher and with any other adults who might be affected, such as the identified Trusted Adult. This group already will have set up the expectations and routines that everyone is agreeing to follow when the student "takes space."

Return — Prepare an apology and/or positive intent and return to class

Before sending the student back to class, make sure they are ready to communicate their positive intent to their teacher, either verbally or in writing. See below for how to set the stage for this. Note: If the student is unable or unwilling to communicate a positive intent, do not send them back to class. Instead, allow them to run through another "recovery" mindfulness practice first. If after that they are still not able to adjust to a more productive mindset, then send them to an administrator.

Setting the stage:

▲ Ask, "How can you communicate to your teacher that you're calm and ready to return and learn? What can you honestly say to your teacher?" Note: A list of prompts might be helpful. This list might include statements, such as, "I am calm and ready to learn," "I am sorry and ready to try again," "I am struggling today, but I did not mean to be disrespectful," "I am sorry I caused a disruption and I will try to not do that again," and "I am still angry, but I will try to be calm and respectful."

▲ Have the student write their positive intent on a piece of paper, or practice it verbally with you. After you send them back to class, fill out an incident log and call parents, if appropriate.

APPENDIX B

Swaddle Interventions
Planning Templates & Samples

The blank planning templates that follow can be downloaded at consciousteaching.com/thiskid/resources

Swaddle Intervention
Phase 1 — Pre-Planning Checklist

Teacher's Name(s): _____

Student's Name: _____

Focus of Intervention: *List or describe the problematic behavior:* _____

_____

_____

▲ I believe that this student wants to do better AND that I can help them do better.

▲ A possible Invisible Subtitle that might go with this student's unproductive behavior might be: _____

▲ I understand that I must change in either thought, action, or both, if I want to effectively support this student in making behavioral changes.

▲ I have chosen a single, concrete, observable, trackable replacement behavior to focus this intervention on. That replacement behavior is: _____

_____

▲ I have a rough plan for how I want to support the student around this behavior. My rough plan has each of the following:

   • An initial stepping-stone goal that is simple and realistically achievable. That goal is: _____

   • A simple tracking system for monitoring the student's daily progress.

   • Two or more incentives/rewards I think might motivate the student. These include: _____

   _____

   • A plan for the use of consequences to support the student's understanding of where the boundaries of acceptable behavior are.

   • One or more things I plan to do differently, or one or more ways in which I plan to interact with the student differently, during this intervention. This/ these will include: _____

   _____

   • A plan for how to do simple and fast daily debriefs or end of day / period check-ins.

Swaddle Intervention
Phase 2 — The Plan

Teacher's Name(s): _____

Student's Name: _____

Focus of Intervention: *List or describe the problematic behavior:* _____
_____
_____
_____
_____

Replacement Behavior: *List or describe the ideal behavior:* _____
_____
_____
_____

Initial Stepping-Stone Goal: *Describe the first, small behavioral change you will support the student in making, in pursuit of ultimately achieving the Replacement Behavior:* _____
_____
_____
_____

Modifications: *What changes will be made in the classroom to support the student in achieving the stepping-stone goal?* _____
_____
_____
_____

Swaddle Intervention: Phase 2 — The Plan: Page 2

Consequences/Redirects: *What consequences will be used, or how will consequences be applied differently, to support the student in achieving the stepping-stone goal?* _____

_____

_____

_____

_____

_____

Teacher Modifications: *What will the teacher do differently to support the student in achieving the stepping-stone goal?* _____

_____

_____

_____

Incentives/Rewards: *What will the student receive each time they accomplish the stepping-stone goal in the coming week?* _____

_____

_____

_____

Tracking: *How will the student's successes and challenges in following the intervention be explicitly tracked?* _____

_____

_____

_____

Daily Check-in: *When and how will brief, simple, daily check-ins occur, so that rewards can be given, progress (or difficulties) acknowledged, and optimism for tomorrow established?* _____

_____

_____

_____

Swaddle Intervention: Phase 2 — The Plan: Page 3

Other Details: *What else needs to be explicitly stated in order to make this intervention successful?* _____

_____

_____

_____

_____

▲   **Practice/Role Play:** Check this box if the teacher and student physically practiced together what each will do differently during this intervention. The practice is intended to mimic what success would look like, how consequences will be applied, and how consequences should be responded to by the student, when success is temporarily out of reach.

Dates for first week of intervention: _____

Reflection Date: *When will we meet again—at the end of the first week—to review, reflect and revise the plan for the following week?* _____

_____

Backup Reflection Date: *If the student or the teacher is unexpectedly not available to meet on the stated reflection date above, what will the backup date be?* _____

_____

Signature of Teacher _____

Signature of Student _____

Swaddle Intervention
Phase 3 — Implementation

Implement the plan for one week, doing brief, daily check-ins. Meet together at the end of the week (or after the first 5 to 7 days of implementation) to discuss successes and challenges, and to make any necessary alterations to the intervention plan.

If things were rough:

▲ Acknowledge, without blaming, that the process was difficult.

▲ Celebrate any successes, no matter how small.

▲ Modify the plan to increase its potential for success.

▲ Be clear about what success will look like, how it will be tracked, what each of you will do differently, and when and how rewards will be given.

▲ Set an optimistic tone for moving forward, and offer a clean slate.

If things went well:

▲ Celebrate the successes, small and large.

▲ Decide whether the goal for the coming week will stay the same—to generate more success—or whether the goal will be modified to make it slightly more difficult to achieve, thus moving to the next stepping-stone goal.

▲ Be clear about what success will now look like, how it will be tracked, and when and how rewards will be given.

▲ Thank the student for their hard work and set a positive tone for the coming week.

If you want a guide for these reflection conversations, you can use the **Swaddle Phase 4 Reflection & Revision** guide, on the following pages. You might use this reflection guide in a variety of ways. Some suggestions are below, but you can decide for yourself what will work best for you and your student.

▲ With older kids, you might consider printing a blank copy for you and another for the student. Have each of you fill it out separately, and then compare notes.

▲ With younger kids, you might consider using a blank copy and filling it in with them, having them give their thoughts and answers before sharing your own.

▲ With a student of any age, you might fill in a copy ahead of time, as preparation for having a reflective conversation with them. It is not necessary to show the student what you have written, if you do not feel it will help them to reflect

Swaddle Intervention
Phase 4 — Reflection & Revision

Reflection for week # *(Circle one):*   1   2   3   4   5   6

Teacher's Name(s): _____

Student's Name: _____

What went well this week? _____

_____

_____

_____

_____

_____

What needs to go better or differently next week? _____

_____

_____

_____

_____

What changes, if any, need to be made to the goal? What is our new goal for next week?

_____

_____

_____

_____

_____

_____

What does the teacher need to do differently, if anything? _____

_____

_____

_____

_____

Swaddle Intervention: Phase 4 — Reflection & Revision: Page 2

What changes, if any, need to be made to the tracking system? _____

_____

_____

_____

_____

_____

What changes, if any, need to be made to the redirects and consequences being used?

_____

_____

_____

_____

_____

What changes, if any, need to be made to how rewards are earned or received? _____

_____

_____

_____

_____

What rewards will be given for achieving the next goal? _____

_____

_____

_____

_____

How can this reflection be ended in a positive and optimistic way? _____

_____

_____

_____

_____

_____

Swaddle Intervention
Sample Plan #1

Elementary School — The Runner

BACKGROUND: Marcus was a 2nd-grader who ran in and out of the classroom without permission, all day long. He was once observed leaving and returning six times in a single hour. In the hallways, he was loud, singing or ranting or banging on lockers. He would get into altercations with other kids who were in the hallway, on their way to or from their own classrooms. He sometimes opened other classroom doors and yelled into the rooms. When told to return to class by other teachers, he would laugh or yell or respond with profanity. When told to return by administrators, he would return, wait a few minutes, and then immediately leave again. He was once found wandering in the parking lot; another time, he was found across the street from the school, trying to climb a lamp post.

This "running" behavior impeded his ability to learn and was also distracting to others, both in his classroom and in other classrooms. It was also unsafe, as he was unsupervised while out of class. Over a two-month period, his recess was taken away repeatedly, classroom privileges were revoked, he was sent to the office, and administrators called his mom. These consequences had no effect on his behavior.

▲   ▲   ▲

Teacher's Name(s): Mr. J.

Student's Name: Marcus

Focus of Intervention:

▲   Marcus runs in and out of the classroom without permission, all day long, every day.

Replacement Behavior:

▲   Marcus will stay in the room, and remain seated, unless he has the teacher's explicit permission to be up and moving.

Initial Stepping-Stone Goal:

▲   Marcus will go to a specific spot in the room, rather than out of the room, when he feels the need to disengage or escape. He will go there without distracting—talking to or touching—others.

▲   He will accomplish this at least twice in a school day. Note: This might be too big a first step for Marcus. If necessary, the goal can be modified so that he needs to remember to run to his spot, instead of out the door, (a) only once in a day, without distracting others, and/or (b) once or twice in a day, even if he is still disruptive to others on his way there.

Swaddle Intervention: Sample Plan #1: Page 2

Modifications:

▲ Marcus will be provided with a safe spot inside the classroom that he can escape to when he feels the need to disengage. He will have specific items in that spot that he can interact with until the teacher has time to come and talk with him, or until he is ready to return to his assigned spot on his own.

▲ A small, pop-up children's play tent will be placed in the back of the room. Inside will be a pillow, blanket, and a locked box that only he knows the combination to. Inside the box will be a selection of toys and other objects he likes, including crayons and paper, a fidget spinner, and some LEGO® guys. This will be his "safe spot."

Consequences/Redirects:

▲ When Marcus runs out of the room, instead of to his safe spot, the following consequences will be applied:

- 1st run-out = Verbal warning, reminder of where he should go, and reminder of what will happen the next time he runs out.
- 2nd run-out = Sent to office for 10+ minutes of time out. Check mark is added to his daily "run chart."
- 3rd run-out = Sent to office for 15+ minutes of time out and talk with admin. Parent called. Second mark added to run chart. Reminded that one more check mark on run chart will result in being sent home for the day.
- 4th run out = Sent home for the day.

Teacher Modifications:

▲ Mr. J. will not ignore the first run-out, and will immediately bring Marcus back, assuming Marcus is just outside the door, which he usually is. Mr. J. will also remind Marcus of where he should go, walk him there, and remind him of what will happen if he again leaves the room without permission.

▲ When interacting with Marcus verbally, Mr. J. will use a calm, kind, and quiet voice and will not display any negative emotion.

▲ Mr. J. will apply the 1–4 consequences consistently, as will the administration, for two weeks before reflecting on its effectiveness.

Incentives/Rewards:

▲ Each time Marcus goes to his spot inside the classroom, he will receive a nonverbal, positive acknowledgement from the teacher, such as a smile or a thumbs up, along with a "star-buck." Star-bucks can be turned in at the end of the day for prizes from the prize box, or they can be saved and accumulated for larger prizes that require more star-bucks.

▲ Any day in which Marcus receives at least one star-buck before lunch, he also will be allowed to eat with his older brother, who is in 5th grade and whom he adores.

Swaddle Intervention: Sample Plan #1: Page 3

Tracking:

▲ Mr. J. will track on a small chart the number of times Marcus "ran out" versus "ran to his spot."

▲ An office administrator will track the number of "run-outs" that result in Marcus's being sent to the office.

Daily Check-in:

▲ During clean up at the end of the day, Mr. J. and Marcus will confer briefly, for no more than two minutes. Mr. J. will acknowledge, without frustration or blame, how many times Marcus successfully "ran to his spot" and how many times he "ran out" of the room. Mr. J. will congratulate him on his hard work, and ask him if he wants to redeem or save any earned star-bucks for a current or later prize. Mr. J. also will set the goal for tomorrow, as well as expressing optimism for Marcus's ability to improve.

▲ Example: "Good job today, Marcus. You had three run-outs but also two run-to-spots. I know it's hard for you to run to your safe spot, so thank you for your hard work there. Do you want to turn in your star-bucks for a small prize or save them for later? I'm looking forward to an even better day tomorrow."

Other Details:

▲ If Marcus is sent home early in the process—which is very likely, as he tests the boundaries of any new system—then Mr. J. will set an optimistic tone when Marcus returns the next day. He will take Marcus aside for a moment, at the beginning of class, and tell him he is looking forward to a better day together. He'll also remind him where his safe spot is, when and how to use it, and what incentives he can earn by using it.

▲ Mr. J. will not require Marcus to make eye contact with him, or to acknowledge him in any way during this conversation. Mr. J. will assume that Marcus hears him, and that Marcus appreciates his efforts, regardless of how Marcus actually behaves.

Student's Thoughts/Contributions:

▲ Marcus says he doesn't care about getting sent home or about getting star-bucks. However, it was his idea to earn eating lunch with his brother, and he seemed genuinely excited about it. It was also his idea to put fidget spinners and LEGO® men in the lock box in his safe spot.

☐ **Practice/Role Play:** Check this box if the teacher and student physically practiced together what each will do differently during this intervention. The practice is intended to mimic what success would look like, how consequences will be applied, and how consequences should be responded to by the student, when success is temporarily out of reach.

Swaddle Intervention: Sample Plan #1: Page 4

Dates for first week of intervention: November 6 – 10

Reflection Date: Friday, November 10, at lunch. Or, if necessary, at the end of the day during the second half of Science. If done during Science, an administrator or the literacy coach will come in to take over the class to free up Mr. J.

Backup Reflection Date: Monday November 13th, before school or at lunch

Signature of Teacher _____

Signature of Student _____

Swaddle Intervention
Sample Plan #2

Elementary School — The Growler

BACKGROUND: Amanda was a 4th-grader who grunted, growled, and hissed when someone got too physically close to her, or when she got upset with peers or adults or herself. If the person she growled at responded in any way, then Amanda would become physically violent and would push, kick, or bite the other person. On one occasion, Amanda threw a full pencil box at another student when the other student growled back at her.

This "growling" behavior impeded the ability of both Amanda and other students to learn. She was easily frustrated—and therefore was growling continually—which others found distracting, annoying, or even intimidating. Through the first half of the school year, Amanda was sent to time-out multiple times every day for this behavior. Her desk was moved to isolate her. She could not work in pairs or groups. She was usually left at her desk when the class was brought to the carpet for mini-lessons. She was suspended twice for acts of violence against other students. Amanda's parents were called weekly and came in three times for conferences. None of the classroom, administrative, or home consequences had any effect on her behavior.

▲ ▲ ▲

Teacher's Name(s): Ms. T.

Student's Name: Amanda

Focus of Intervention:

▲ Amanda growls and sometimes attacks others when uncomfortable, upset, frustrated, or overwhelmed.

Replacement Behavior:

▲ Amanda will use appropriate words and tone to express her feelings of discomfort.

Initial Stepping-Stone Goal:

▲ Amanda will use an image to express her upset and then remove herself from tense situations without attacking/touching others.

▲ Amanda will accomplish this at least once while at the carpet or working in a group with her classmates.

Swaddle Intervention: Sample Plan #2: Page 2

Modifications:

▲ Amanda will be given a laminated card to wear around her neck on a lanyard with an image that represents anger. Amanda will choose this image from a selection provided by Ms. T., or Amanda can suggest an image.

▲ When Amanda gets triggered and wants to growl, she will instead hold the image up to the person she is frustrated with and then move to another location in the room—either her desk or a designated beanbag chair, whichever is further away from where the upset occurs.

Consequences/Redirects:

▲ When Amanda growls, Ms. T. will remind her to show her lanyard image instead.

- If Amanda complies—and shows the image to the person she growled at—then Ms. T. will give her a thumbs-up. Ms. T. will point to Amanda's desk or the beanbag chair to indicate nonverbally that she should now go to that location to cool down. Amanda can stay there until she is ready to return to the activity, or until the teacher has time to check in with her, or until the class transitions to the next activity. Even though Amanda growled, her incentive/reward is earned for this compliance.

- If Amanda does not comply—and instead now growls at Ms. T.—then Ms. T. will point to Amanda's desk or the beanbag chair to indicate nonverbally that she should now go to that location to cool down.

  - If Amanda goes to the indicated location, then Ms. T. will debrief with her later, thank her for moving when asked, and remind her how to use the card in the future.

  - If Amanda refuses to move, then the students around her will be moved away from her instead. During the teacher's next break in the day (recess, lunch, specials, or free-choice time), Amanda and Ms. T. will have a private conversation. Ms. T. will again remind Amanda of how to use the lanyard image, how to move when asked, and what incentives are attached. She will ask Amanda if she wants the teacher to do anything differently to support her in this effort. Ms. T. will end by providing Amanda with a clean slate.

  - If Amanda physically attacks another student or destroys property in the classroom, then she will be sent to the office. Admin will call her parent. If warranted, Amanda will be suspended. If not warranted, Amanda will be sent back to class when, and only when, she states that she is ready to make amends and has a plan for doing so. This might be a written or verbal apology to the student she pushed. Or it might be organizing or cleaning up an area she attempted to destroy.

Swaddle Intervention: Sample Plan #2: Page 3

Teacher Modifications:

▲   Ms. T. will not take away recess or lunch or specials as a punishment. However, the beginnings of these periods can be used occasionally, when necessary, to have private conversations and/or briefly practice the stepping-stone goal. But after the talk or practice, Amanda will be sent to join her classmates.

▲   Ms. T. will use nonverbal gestures to indicate when Amanda should move to another location, instead of telling her verbally.

Incentives/Rewards:

▲   When Amanda shows the card to someone, whether or not she growls at the same time, and then removes herself to her appointed seat, whether or not she has to be reminded to go, she earns one small item from the classroom store.

▲   When Amanda uses the card INSTEAD of growling OR removes herself to her assigned seat WITHOUT BEING REMINDED, she earns one medium to large item from the classroom store.

▲   When Amanda uses the card instead of growling AND removes herself to her assigned seat without being reminded, she earns first choice in choosing next week's class jobs.

▲   When Amanda completes an entire day without growling, she earns pizza lunch with Mrs. Q. from the main office.

Tracking:

▲   Ms. T. will track growling, card use, and removal to assigned seat on a clipboard.

Daily Check-in:

▲   During free-choice time at end of day, Ms. T. will check in with Amanda and let her choose prizes from the class store, as appropriate.

Other Details: None.

Student's Thoughts/Contributions:

▲   While we discussed the plan, Amanda initially was silent and would not make eye contact. However, when we got to incentives, she had a lot to say; she was chatty and engaged when selecting the image for the lanyard card. She also enjoyed practicing using the card before we left the meeting.

☐   **Practice/Role Play:** Check this box if the teacher and student physically practiced together what each will do differently during this intervention. The practice is intended to mimic what success would look like, how consequences will be applied, and how consequences should be responded to by the student, when success is temporarily out of reach.

Swaddle Intervention: Sample Plan #2: Page 4

Dates for first week of intervention: January 15 – 19

Reflection Date: January 19, during free choice time at end of day

Backup Reflection Date: January 22, before school or during morning free-write

Signature of Teacher   _____

Signature of Student   _____

Swaddle Intervention
Sample Plan #3

Secondary School — The Arguer

BACKGROUND: Brianna was an 8th-grader who argued whenever she was told to do something she didn't want to do, or whenever she was told to stop doing something she didn't want to stop doing. She was confrontational, combative, and oppositional almost all the time. Every interaction sparked a debate or a battle. Simple things, such as, "Please sit down, class has begun," would set her off. She would yell a response, voice dripping with attitude. "I'm going to my seat! Don't you have eyes?" or "I'll get there when I get there!" or "You go to your seat!" or "Why are you picking on me? I'm not the only one standing up right now!" These types of responses were completely predictable, default modes of her expression; they also represented the milder end of her spectrum when interacting with teachers. She was particularly volatile with her math teacher, whom she once stalked around the room while screaming invectives. On that occasion, she was forcibly removed from the class by campus security.

Brianna's oppositional behavior impeded her and her classmates' ability to learn, as well as the teacher's ability to teach. Private conversations, detention, loss of classroom and schoolwide privileges, phone calls home, visits to the office, failing grades, offers of incentives, and attempts to personally connect and meet her defiance with kindness had no noticeable impact on her behavior.

▲   ▲   ▲

Teacher's Name(s): Ms. G.

Student's Name: Brianna

Focus of Intervention:

▲   Brianna meets all reasonable requests or directives with confrontation and arguing. While she usually, ultimately, complies with requests, her compliance is accompanied by loud and dramatic scenes that absorb instructional time and create a tense and difficult learning environment for all those around her.

Replacement Behavior:

▲   Brianna will comply with reasonable teacher requests without resistance or upset.

Initial Stepping-Stone Goal:

▲   Brianna will comply with one teacher request per period without any verbal response.

Swaddle Intervention: Sample Plan #3: Page 2

Modifications: N/A

Consequences/Redirects:

▲ When Brianna verbally argues with a request from Ms. G., then Ms. G. will hold up both her hands, palms facing Brianna, as a signal to "stop." Then she will nonverbally repeat the request. For example, she might point to Brianna's seat, if the request was to sit, or opening her hands like a book, if the request was to read.

- If Brianna complies, then she earns an incentive—even if she started out arguing, even if she grumbles quietly to herself, even if her body language is aggressive, and even if she bangs materials.
- If Brianna does not comply, and continues to verbally argue, then Ms. G. will soften her eyes, lower her voice, and offer Brianna a choice to comply with the request or receive a consequence. Depending on the request and situation, consequences might include:
  - Being removed from a group or pair.
  - Being sent outside to cool off for a moment.
  - After-school or lunch detention, during which the behavior will be discussed.
  - Being sent to the office, her counselor, or another location/person on campus to decompress.

Teacher Modifications:

▲ Ms. G. will not engage in verbal debates or arguments with Brianna. She will not explain or give reasons for why she is asking Brianna to be on task.

▲ Ms. G. will not ignore Brianna when Brianna does not comply, but will rather follow the consequences plan listed above: non-verbal "stop" signal, non-verbal request to be on task, verbal choice offered with soft voice, soft eyes, and positive intent, and consequence, if necessary.

▲ Ms. G. will use detention only as an opportunity to connect with Brianna, to debrief regarding her progress, or to practice the stepping-stone goal with her. Detention will last only as long as is necessary to complete this connection, debrief, or practice. Brianna will not be left to sit in silence or told to complete academic work during this detention.

Incentives/Rewards:

▲ Each time Brianna complies with any request without arguing, or stops arguing and complies after the teacher repeats the request nonverbally, she can reduce her homework for that night by half. So if she complies with 2 requests, she receives no homework that night. She earns this reward whether or not she later argues with other requests during the same period.

▲ Each time Brianna goes an entire period without arguing, or stops arguing immediately upon every request, she earns a 10-minute early release to eat lunch with a friend of her choosing, plus no homework.

Swaddle Intervention: Sample Plan #3: Page 3

Tracking:

▲ Ms. G. will track arguing versus non-arguing compliance using hash marks on a two-column chart on her desk.

Daily Check-in:

▲ At the end of each period, Ms. G. will write Brianna a note indicating the number of argues versus non-argues, and the accompanying homework reduction. She will also acknowledge Brianna's effort. For example, "Brianna, today you complied without arguing 1 time and argued 7 times. That means you can cut your homework by half! Great job! There are 8 questions for homework. Please choose the odds or evens to complete. I really appreciate your hard work today. Looking forward to tomorrow.☺" Or, "Brianna, today you argued every one of the 5 times I asked you to be on task. That means your homework is the same as everyone else's tonight. But trying to break a habit is hard work. It takes time and patience. I know you can do it. Looking forward to tomorrow.☺"

Other Details: None.

Student's Thoughts/Contributions:

▲ Brianna presented an attitude of disgust during the entire meeting. She tried several times to blame Ms. G. for why she had to argue with her. And she felt that a 1/4 reduction in homework (the original incentive proposed by Ms. G.) was unfair, and that she should receive no homework if she agreed to "put up with" Ms. G. A compromise was struck at 1/2 off homework each time she complied without arguing.

☐ **Practice/Role Play:** Check this box if the teacher and student physically practiced together what each will do differently during this intervention. The practice is intended to mimic what success would look like, how consequences will be applied, and how consequences should be responded to by the student, when success is temporarily out of reach.

Dates for first week of intervention: October 23 – 27

Reflection Date: October 27, at lunch or during Ms. G.'s prep period

Backup Reflection Date: October 30, before school or during Ms. G.'s prep period

Signature of Teacher _____

Signature of Student _____

Swaddle Intervention
Sample Plan #4

Secondary School — The Wanderer

BACKGROUND: Michael was an 11th-grader who would not stay seated for more than a few minutes at a time in his English class. Whenever he felt compelled, he would get up, wander about the room, and talk with other students in a loud and animated way, even if the teacher was talking. When asked to return to his seat, he would ignore the request, acting as if he did not hear the teacher, and continue to wander and disrupt. No matter how many times his English teacher called his name, Michael would never acknowledge that the teacher spoke. If the teacher walked over to him and stood next to him to try and get his attention, he would still ignore the teacher. If the teacher tapped his shoulder or touched him gently to get his attention, Michael would simply walk away, wait for the teacher to continue teaching, and then start talking to someone else. Michael was, on the surface, a disruptive but good-natured class-clown when left to his own devices. However, if the teacher cornered him, he would stand, mute, staring directly at the teacher, his body shaking with barely controlled rage, and wait for the teacher to walk away. If told to leave the room, then he would ignore, make a joke, or in some other way passively refuse, and he would have to be taken out by campus security or an administrator. When left on his own to wander and disrupt as he liked, he would eventually come back to his seat for short periods of time, but never upon request from the teacher.

Michael's wandering and disruptive behavior impeded his and his classmates' ability to learn, as well as the teacher's ability to teach. Private conversations, detention, phone calls home, visits to the office, and failing grades had no impact on his attitude or behavior.

▲   ▲   ▲

Teacher's Name(s): Mr. S.

Student's Name: Michael

Focus of Intervention:

▲   Michael leaves his seat without permission multiple times every day during English class. He then disrupts the learning by talking/joking loudly with others. When asked to sit or leave the room, he ignores the request.

Replacement Behavior:

▲   Michael will stay seated and focus on his own work during English.

Swaddle Intervention: Sample Plan #4: Page 2

Initial Stepping-Stone Goal:

▲   At least once in a period, Michael will wander to a specific spot designated in the back of the room, taking a designated route to get there and back, without talking to any other students. And/or, if Michael does not use his approved route, or he talks to others while up, he will be asked to return to his seat, which he will do immediately.

Modifications:

▲   Michael will be provided with a clipboard, which will hang in the back of the room. This clipboard is for his exclusive use, so that he can do work while standing there. He can wander from the clipboard to his seat and back as he feels necessary, by taking a specific route. If Mr. S. needs to ask him to return to his seat, when possible Mr. S. will walk by him and show him a card that says "return to your seat." When not possible, Mr. S. will call Michael's name and gesture toward his seat using an open hand.

Consequences/Redirects:

▲   When Michael wanders off his route, or when he talks to others while on his route, Mr. S. will get his attention by calling his name or tapping him on the shoulder, and then nonverbally request that Michael return to his seat.

   •   If Michael complies, and returns immediately to his seat without having to be asked again, then he earns an incentive, even if he was off-route and/or talking to others.

   •   If Michael ignores Mr. S.'s request, then Mr. S. will ask Michael to step outside the room for a brief conversation

      •   If he goes outside, then Mr. S. will use a calm voice to remind Michael of the plan, what Michael's part is, and the incentive for cooperation. Mr. S. will then ask Michael to enter the room when, and only when, he is ready to walk quietly to his chair, sit, and try again. Mr. S. will then re-enter class. If Michael does not come in and sit within 5 minutes, then Mr. S. will write him a referral to the office.

      •   If Michael refuses to go outside, then Mr. S. will write him a referral to the office and call for an escort to take him out of class.

Teacher Modifications:

▲   Mr. S. will not require Michael to verbally acknowledge any of his requests. Nonverbal compliance will be sufficient.

▲   Mr. S. will not require Michael to be in his seat at all, as long as Michael is quietly on his route or at his place in the back of the room.

▲   Mr. S. will not call Michael out in front of the class to get his attention, unless absolutely necessary. Mr. S. will use nonverbal gestures or images to request that Michael return to his seat

▲   Mr. S. will follow the consequences plan listed above.

Swaddle Intervention: Sample Plan #4: Page 3

Incentives/Rewards:

▲ The first time in any week that Michael makes it through an entire period without ignoring Mr. S.'s requests, and without disturbing others when Mr. S. asks him to return to his assigned seat, Michael will earn an extra bathroom/homework pass.

▲ Each week that Michael follows the plan successfully for 3 or more days, Michael will earn a 10-minute early release from school that Friday.

▲ When Michael follows the plan successfully for 4 or more days in each of three successive weeks, he earns two free tickets to the prom.

Tracking:

▲ Mr. S. will track three things: (1) How often Michael goes to or from his clipboard on-route without talking; (2) How often Michael immediately cooperates when asked to return to his seat for being off-route or for talking on-route; (3) How often Michael does not cooperate when asked to return to his seat for being off-route or for talking on-route.

Daily Check-in:

▲ At the end of each period, Mr. S. will have a brief, private meeting with Michael, show him the chart, acknowledge any success, and give rewards earned. He will offer a clean slate and say he is looking forward to tomorrow.

Other Details: None.

Student's Thoughts/Contributions:

▲ Michael was silent throughout the meeting. He spoke only when asked if he would be interested in any of the offered incentives. Free prom tickets was his suggestion and was added as a large incentive for a future goal.

☐ **Practice/Role Play:** Check this box if the teacher and student physically practiced together what each will do differently during this intervention. The practice is intended to mimic what success would look like, how consequences will be applied, and how consequences should be responded to by the student, when success is temporarily out of reach.

Dates for first week of intervention: February 19 – 23

Reflection Date: February 23, after school

Backup Reflection Date: February 26, before school or during Mr. S.'s prep period

Signature of Teacher _____

Signature of Student _____

APPENDIX C

Recommended Books on Bias & Equity

Excellence Through Equity: Five Principles of Courageous Leadership to Guide Achievement for Every Student
Alan M. Blankstein & Pedro Noguera, with Lorena Kelly
Foreword by Archbishop Desmond Tutu
Alexandria, VA: ASCD (2016)
ISBN: 978-1416622505

Building Equity: Policies and Practices to Empower All Learners
Dominique Smith, Nancy Frey, Ian Pumpian, & Douglas Fisher
Alexandria, VA: ASCD (2017)
ISBN: 978-1416624264

How to Teach Kids Who Don't Look Like you: Culturally Responsive Teaching Strategies
Bonnie M. Davis
Thousand Oaks, CA: Corwin, SAGE Publications Ltd. (2012)
ISBN: 978-1452257914

Teaching with Poverty in Mind: What Being Poor Does to Kids' Brains and What Schools Can Do About It
Eric Jensen
Alexandria, VA: ASCD (2009)
ISBN: 978-1416608844

A Framework for Understanding Poverty: A Cognitive Approach, 6th Edition
Ruby K. Payne, PhD
Highlands, TX: Aha! Process, Inc. (2018)
ISBN: 978-1938248016

APPENDIX D

Sample Reflection Sheets

The sample reflection sheets that follow can be downloaded at consciousteaching.com/thiskid/resources

_____'s Think Sheet

I can think about my choices and how they affect ME and others.

What I chose to do:

kick	hit	push	bite	talk or scream

run	not work	pinch	use unkind words	throw something

It made _____ feel:

happy	sad	mad	scared	frustrated

Next time I can choose to:

have SAFE feet	have SAFE hands	use kind words	listen and not talk during instruction	ask for a calm break

say "I need space."	ask someone to "Please stop."	follow directions	stay in my work area	say, "I don't understand."

When I make a positive choice like that:

others will want to be with me	others will feel good around me	others want to play with me	people will know that I am kind	I will feel proud of myself

Source:

http://www.mypbis.org/wp-content/uploads/2012/04/Visual-Think-Sheet.pdf

3rd, 4th and 5th Grade Think Sheet

Name: _____

Date: _____

1. What expectation did I not meet?

_____

_____

_____

_____

2. Why was my behavior a problem? (Continue on back if needed.)

_____

_____

_____

_____

3. What could I have done instead? (Continue on back if needed.)

_____

_____

_____

_____

4. Do you need to apologize to anyone?   Did I apologize?

   ☐ Yes   ☐ No   ☐ Yes   ☐ No

   To whom? _____

_____   _____   _____
Student's Signature   Teacher's Signature   Parent/Guardian's Signature

Source:
http://polkdhsd7.sharpschool.com/UserFiles/Servers/Server_3751710/File/D7%20PBS%20
Behavior%20Intervention%20Website%20Resources/Reflection%20Sheet%203rd-5th.pdf

Sample Secondary Reflection Sheet

▲ Write your answers to the questions below.

▲ When done, return to your class and/or assigned seat.

▲ Sit silently and complete your work or read until your teacher comes to talk with you.

Your Name: _____

Period: _____ Teacher: _____

1. What did your teacher ask you to do that you did not, would not, or could not do? Or, what set of circumstances led to you being asked to complete this reflection sheet?

_____

_____

_____

_____

2. What could you have done differently so that your teacher would not have needed to ask you to complete this reflection?

_____

_____

_____

_____

3. This time, your consequence for your inappropriate actions was to complete this reflection sheet. If you are inappropriate in a similar way in the future, what do you think the best consequence would be?

_____

_____

_____

_____

4. What else do you want your teacher to know about what happened or why it happened?

_____

_____

_____

_____

APPENDIX E

Teaching with Trauma in Mind

How Trauma & Toxic Stress Affect Teaching & Learning

Below you will find information and resources for both educating and supporting teachers who work with traumatized youth. The information is organized around four main topics:

1. What Trauma Is & What It Does to Developing Brains
2. How Trauma Affects Classroom Learning
3. How Teachers Can Support Traumatized Students
4. How Working with Traumatized Youth Affects Teachers

A companion PowerPoint for sharing this information can be found at: consciousteaching.com/thiskid/resources.

1. WHAT TRAUMA IS AND WHAT IT DOES TO DEVELOPING BRAINS

▲ Defining terms: Trauma, PTSD, Toxic Stress

▲ Effects of Trauma on Brain Development

Trauma

Trauma can be defined as a psycho-emotional response to an event or an experience that is deeply distressing or disturbing. Trauma often occurs when a person objectively or subjectively experiences a threat to their life or bodily integrity, or a threat to the life or bodily integrity of a caregiver, family member, or other known person. Trauma may be episodic (e.g., a natural disaster, the death of a loved one, being witness to or the victim of a violent attack) or chronic (e.g., chronic abuse or neglect, sexual abuse, poverty, threats of deportation).

Post-Traumatic Stress Disorder (PTSD)

PTSD is a psychiatric diagnosis that includes a collection of symptoms that people develop in response to a traumatic event—something they witnessed or experienced. Common symptoms include:

▲ Re-experiencing the event through nightmares and/or flashbacks.

▲ Avoiding people, places, or things that remind them of the event.

▲ Dissociating (spacing out) and/or emotional numbness.

▲ Heightened emotional state experienced as frequently feeling irritable, jumpy, or on edge,

▲ Difficulty sleeping.

Toxic Stress:

People are described as living with toxic stress when they live in situations that involve **ongoing** severe stressors or traumatic situations, such as poverty, abuse, neglect, exposure to violence, and/or living with a caregiver with untreated substance abuse or mental health issues.

Toxic Stress and the Brain:

The persistent stress caused by experiencing ongoing trauma changes brain architecture, resulting in underdeveloped neural connections in areas of the brain most important for successful learning and behavior in school. This underdevelopment impacts reasoning, planning, and impulse control, and also creates an overproduction of neural connections in the areas of the brain involved in fear, anxiety, and impulsiveness.

When we experience a threat, the rational part of our brains shuts down as the Sympathetic Nervous System engages, flooding the bloodstream with adrenaline and cortisol. This creates a heightened state of alertness that prepares our bodies to fight, flee, or freeze. This response is meant to be short-lived to help us survive an immediate threat. Once the threat is dealt with, our Parasympathetic Nervous System takes over and brings us back to our resting state, where our rational brain can again take over. When someone is living with ongoing, daily stressors or threats, their Sympathetic Nervous System is being overactivated, which not only impairs rational thinking and the ability to focus, learn, and remember, but also compromises the immune system. Consequently, children living with toxic stress are not only more likely to struggle academically and behaviorally, but they are also more likely to be chronically ill.

Links to references, research, and resources on this topic can be found at www.consciousteaching.com/thiskid/resources.

2. HOW TRAUMA AFFECTS STUDENTS IN SCHOOL

▲ How Toxic Stress Affects Learning

▲ Manifestations & Coping Mechanisms

Trauma & Learning

Trauma and toxic stress can strongly impact brain development, dramatically affecting student learning and behavior in school. Specifically, students experiencing trauma show earlier and more pronounced development in the limbic system (the "reactionary" part of the brain), whereas neurotypical students' brains prioritize early development in the cerebral cortexes (the "thinking/reasoning" part of the brain).

When children grow up in a non-threatening environment, their early brain growth is focused primarily on the development of cognition and socio-emotional skills. During childhood, development of the self-regulation and survival-skill parts of the brain take a backseat. For students experiencing adversity, however, this development is reversed, with survival and regulatory skills necessarily taking precedence over the development of cognitive and socio-emotional skills. Consequently, students living with trauma and/or toxic stress are less likely to develop the academic and social skills necessary to thrive in a school setting, skills such as:

- ▲ problem solving
- ▲ language and communication
- ▲ understanding cause-and-effect relationships
- ▲ sequential organization

Coping Behaviors

Since students who experience trauma operate under the assumption that the world is a dangerous place, they might also exhibit defensive behaviors that they have developed over time to protect themselves from physical or psychological harm. These mechanisms help them cope with the continual stress they experience, but they also impede their ability to function productively in a school setting: These often include:

- ▲ Physical symptoms (e.g., headaches and stomachaches).
- ▲ Unpredictable and/or impulsive behavior.
- ▲ Overreacting or underreacting to environmental stimuli (e.g., bells, physical contact, sirens).
- ▲ Intense reactions to reminders of a past trauma.
- ▲ Feeling as though personal space is being violated.
- ▲ Blowing up when corrected or told what to do by an a uthority figure.

Manifestations of Toxic Stress

As students grow older, they tend to cope with toxic stress in one of two ways:

1. Avoidance, which manifests as low motivation and/or emotional numbing.

2. Hyperarousal, which manifests as low impulse control and/or explosive emotions.

As a result of their abnormal brain development and their overloaded Sympathetic Nervous Systems, children and teens living with toxic stress, or experiencing traumatic events, tend to have difficulty with:

- ▲ sitting still

- ▲ staying on task / concentrating

- ▲ paying attention

- ▲ regulating emotions

- ▲ feeling empathy

- ▲ interacting with others appropriately

- ▲ managing impulses

Links to references, research, and resources on this topic can be found at www.consciousteaching.com/thiskid/resources.

3. WHAT TEACHERS CAN DO FOR TRAUMATIZED YOUTH

- ▲ What Teachers Should Not Do

- ▲ What Teachers Can Do

- ▲ Proof That Positive Outcomes Are Possible

How Teachers Sometimes Make Things Worse

When a student begins to display outward signs of going into crisis mode or acting out behaviorally, what teachers don't do is just as important as what they do. Strategies that may be effective with a neurotypical child could actually escalate the situation with a traumatized student, because traumatized students tend to have difficulty accessing the areas of the brain (cerebral cortex, frontal lobe) that deal with logic, reasoning, and judgement.

Intervening with Traumatized Youth

Ineffective / Escalatory Strategies	Effective / Supportive Strategies
▲ Threats	▲ Slowing down
▲ Attempts to increase teacher control	▲ Breathing
▲ Excessive questioning	▲ Connecting with the student
▲ Lecturing	▲ Showing empathy and understanding
▲ Ignoring the behavior	▲ Validating and showing acceptance
▲ Time out	▲ Using non-threatening body language
▲ Point charts	▲ Reducing the power differential

When Teachers Shut Down

When teachers are not aware of the underlying trauma that might be causing students to act out or shut down, they sometimes become frustrated and then shut down themselves. These teachers can be heard saying dismissive things about their most difficult student, such as:

1. He/she just doesn't care.

2. He/she just doesn't have anything going on upstairs.

3. He/she is just a sociopath.

Let's address each of these statements from a trauma-informed perspective:

1. **He/she just doesn't care.** Almost all humans care about their survival and their happiness, and we must assume that our students really do care. The inability to express that care, and the presence of behaviors that seem to indicate otherwise, are

almost always the result of growing up with toxic stress. But more importantly, it is not our students' job to prove to us that they care. It is our job to prove to them that we care, in our every word and action. That is what we signed up for when we chose to enter the teaching profession.

2. **He/she just doesn't have anything going on upstairs.** Numbing and avoidant behaviors are coping mechanisms that children experiencing toxic stress use to protect themselves from fracturing pychologically or emotionally. While these coping mechanisms are often misinterpreted as a lack of intelligence, they are actually indicators that the student doesn't feel safe. If they shut down and tune out, then they can temporarily feel safe from the dangerous world that surrounds them.

3. **He/she is just a sociopath.** Sociopathic behavior is generally used to refer to someone who is both manipulative and also unfeeling. When teachers use this term to describe students, they are usually referring to youth who seem to display conduct disorders or the precursors of Antisocial Personality Disorder. These students might dismiss the rights of others, lie to get what they want, reject rules, appear unaffected by consequences, and lack remorse for their behavior. They might also appear charming and/or emotionally cold — or they might be impulsive, aggressive, reckless, and irresponsible.

   While these behaviors might indicate a current or future mental health diagnosis, statistically this is actually incredibly unlikely. Most of the time these behaviors are in fact just ways that students are responding to toxic stress and trauma. And unlike someone who is actually suffering from Antisocial Personality Disorder, the effects of toxic stress and trauma can be managed and even reversed. Therefore, labeling a student as a "sociopath"—even in our own minds—is not only inaccurate, it is also detrimental. When teachers do this, they give themselves permission to give up on the student, because they have diagnosed the student with a permanent disorder that can't be altered. The truth, however, is that there are many things teachers can do to help reverse the negative behavioral effects of toxic stress in their students.

How Teachers Can Help

As the brain continues to grow and develop throughout childhood, the negative effects of trauma and toxic stress can be minimized if the sources of stress are removed or become less frequent. These positive effects may not be immediately apparent, but they are definitely real and documentable. Studies have proven that when students spend more time in a consistently safe, resiliency-building environment than they do in a traumatic, stressful environment, the underdeveloped parts of their brains can recover and grow. Students spend approximately eight of their sixteen waking hours at school. If their home environment is unsafe or toxic, we can help them and their brains by having their school environment be safe and nurturing.

Teachers and others in the school setting can do a lot to help support traumatized students. First, and most importantly, teachers must recognize and acknowledge that traumatized students may act out because of their changed brain architecture or chemistry rather than out of disrespect or defiance. Only by seeking to understand the needs of a traumatized child can an educator begin to help. An excellent first step is to shift one's mindset from "What's wrong with this kid" to "What's happened to this kid?"

▲ **Build strong personal relationships** with students. One of the best ways to help a child to build resiliency, feel safe, and grow the learning parts of their brain is by creating meaningful, caring relationships with them. Be aware, though, that a student who experiences trauma or toxic stress may have difficulty trusting others. They may be wary of someone being nice/kind/supportive. Continue to be genuinely interested in them and try to develop a personal bond no matter what roadblocks they may thrown up to dissuade you.

▲ **Establish routines** that create a safe and consistent classroom environment. One way to achieve this is by creating calm, predictable transitions in the classroom. Kids with trauma experience a lot of chaos and unpredictable behavior in their home lives. A classroom that has a regular schedule and clear, consistently enforced rules creates a safe environment where they can allow themselves to let their guard down. In addition, it is extremely helpful to prepare kids ahead of time for transitions and changes to the regular bell schedule.

▲ **Give choices instead of directives.** Kids with adverse experiences feel out of control or powerless most of the time. Letting them choose among appropriate choices gives them a sense of control, even when those choices include a directive and a consequence, such as: "You can complete your work now or you can come in at lunch and complete it then. What do you want to do?"

▲ **Practice emotional regulation skills.** Weave into your daily instruction some breathing exercises, stretching, or mindfulness activities. These are particularly powerful and helpful after major transitions, when energy in the room is high and potential triggers lurk everywhere. Or build a writing prompt, art project, or class discussion around the awareness and management of emotions.

▲ **Verbally acknowledge** when a student is doing something positive. Try to find something positive to say to your most vulnerable students at least twice in every hour. Many students living with trauma hear nothing but negativity, judgement, or criticism from adults all day long—things like: "Stop that. What's the matter with you? That's enough!" To have students perceive you as someone who cares, they need to hear more positivity from you than critique. A good rule of thumb is to shoot for three positive things for every one critique or redirect.

▲ **Redirect behavior privately** and in a calm voice. Some students may associate criticism with getting in trouble, which can mean harsh punishment at home. Or they may feel scared to get an answer wrong. Discussing privately gives them an opportunity to manage any feelings that come up in a safer way.

▲ **Notice when a student might be feeling triggered** or going into survival mode—faster breathing, red face, clenched fists, especially quiet demeanor, head down, disengagement from task, deer-in-the-headlights look, agitated fidgeting, or bursting into tears, for example. Privately ask how they are doing or **suggest something that would help them regulate** their mood, such as getting a drink of water, walking to the back of the class and taking some deep breaths, placing their hands flat on their heart and stomach and focusing on the feeling of their breath rising and falling, or writing in a journal.

Proof That It Works

El Dorado Elementary began using trauma-informed and restorative practices in 2009. By 2012–2013 they saw suspensions drop 89%. There were 675 referrals to the principal's office in 2008-2009, and only 175 referrals in 2012–2013.

- https://acestoohigh.com/2014/01/28/hearts-el-dorado-elementary/

At Lincoln High School in Washington State, they began using trauma-informed resilience practices in 2010.

In 2009–2010 (Before new approach)

▲ 798 suspensions (days students were out of school)

▲ 50 expulsions

▲ 600 written referrals

In 2010–2011 (After new approach)

▲ 135 suspensions (days students were out of school)

▲ 30 expulsions

▲ 320 written referrals

- https://acestoohigh.com/2012/04/23/lincoln-high-school-in-walla-walla-wa-tries-new-approach-to-school-discipline-expulsions-drop-85/

Links to references, research, and resources on this topic can be found at www.consciousteaching.com/thiskid/resources.

4. HOW WORKING WITH TRAUMATIZED YOUTH AFFECTS TEACHERS

- ▲ How Teachers Develop Chronic Stress and Vicarious Trauma
- ▲ What Teachers Can Do About Their Vicarious Trauma
- ▲ How Administrators Can Help Teachers

Teachers & Vicarious Trauma

All teachers who work with students affected by trauma and toxic stress are vulnerable to experiencing vicarious trauma. Vicarious trauma, sometimes also referred to as secondary traumatic stress, refers to the effects of hearing about others' trauma, pain, or suffering, and being preoccupied with it. This phenomenon can sometimes also lead to "compassion fatigue"—a numbing, desensitization, minimizing, or loss of empathy for others who are experiencing ongoing trauma—as well as activation of trauma from their own lives, which can be stimulated by the students' stories.

What Teachers Can Do

One of the most important steps in dealing with vicarious trauma and compassion fatigue is to recognize them. Once this is accomplished, a variety of actions and strategies can be used to help counter their effects. Look for signs that you might be experiencing vicarious trauma or compassion fatigue. These might include:

- ▲ Feeling helpless/hopeless.
- ▲ Feeling one can never do enough.
- ▲ Hypervigilance, constant alertness to threats.
- ▲ Diminished creativity.
- ▲ Minimizing, isolating, or blaming others.
- ▲ Chronic exhaustion / physical ailments.
- ▲ Inability to listen / chronic avoidance.
- ▲ Anger and cynicism.

▲ Numbing / Inability to empathize.

▲ Isolation or avoidance.

▲ Loss of pleasure in hobbies and other activities.

▲ Intrusive thoughts about student experiences.

If you think that you or someone else in your school might be experiencing vicarious trauma, here are some self-care things you can do.

▲ **Talk to Others.** Individuals experiencing vicarious trauma, or reactivation of their own trauma as a result of student experiences, are encouraged to talk about it with a trusted friend or colleague rather than trying to ignore it or minimize it. Some teachers might also need professional help, such as consultation with a mental health counselor.

▲ **Take Mental & Physical Breaks.** Teachers should seek out opportunities to give themselves a mental or physical break from working with, or thinking about, their traumatized students. This could be something as simple as taking a break during the workday, allowing oneself to cry, or spending a few minutes each day in engaging in mindfulness or meditation practices. Other self-care strategies include eating and sleeping well, exercising regularly, and engaging in fun activities outside of work.

What Administrators Can Do

In schools with large numbers of youth experiencing trauma, numerous staff members will be at risk for vicarious trauma and compassion fatigue. Administrators and school leaders can take steps to support their staff in dealing with these issues.

First and foremost, school leaders must acknowledge, appreciate, and address the reality and impact of vicarious stress. Studies indicate that teachers in schools where their leadership acknowledges, names, and takes proactive steps to support staff around vicarious trauma show dramatic improvements in teacher morale, enthusiasm, and job satisfaction. In addition, there is an acompanying reduction in teacher absenteeism and negative talk about students, the school, and the community.

▲ **Positive Talk & Connections.** School leaders can increase positive connections between themselves and staff by celebrating things that are going well and highlighting situations where staff are having success with their most challenging students. Calling out these positive interactions, either privately (in person or by email with a teacher) or publicly (at a staff meeting or email to all staff), can help teachers to feel seen, understood, and appreciated. This care, shown by leadership, will in turn help teachers to better care for their students. Just as with students, school leaders should shoot for highlighting three positive things teachers are doing as they work with traumatized youth for every one critique they give or for every one change they request.

▲ **Wellness Groups.** School leaders can create a wellness group for staff to take part in. Weekly or monthly optional wellness group meetings might include opportunities for teachers to talk about their feelings and experiences, practice calming techniques, or engage together in relaxing physical activities, such as stretching or walking.

▲ **Mindfulness in Staff Meetings.** School leaders can start staff meetings with a wellness practice, such as meditative breathing, expressing gratitude for teachers, highlighting good things happening in classrooms, having teachers express gratitude for one another, or modeling mindfulness techniques.

Links to references, research, and resources on this topic can be found at www.consciousteaching.com/thiskid/resources.

ABOUT THE AUTHORS

Grace Dearborn

Grace Dearborn is an education consultant, author, instructional coach, award-winning teacher, and international presenter on classroom management, brain-compatible teaching, motivating reluctant learners, and instructional coaching. She has been in education for over 20 years, and for most of that time she taught at-risk teens in the San Francisco Bay Area. In addition to being a veteran classroom teacher, Grace has worked as a mentor teacher, literacy coach, curriculum developer, and professional development coordinator. Currently, Grace is the Executive Director of Conscious Teaching, LLC. In this role she spends most of her time running herself ragged coordinating and facilitating workshops for teachers across the United States and internationally. And she loves every minute of it! She also assists administrators in making schoolwide discipline-system changes and assists mentors and instructional coaches in improving their support for new and struggling teachers. In her free time she volunteers at local schools, reads voraciously, bakes emotionally, plays tennis and poker competently (or so she likes to believe), and spends as much time as possible with her family, where her skills at motivating and managing youth are daily put to their truest test by her two teenaged sons.

Scott Sturgeon

Dr. Scott Sturgeon is currently a principal supervisor and coach, and formerly worked as a principal, assistant principal, classroom teacher, and paraprofessional. He has been in education for 20 years and spent all of that time in an urban, high-poverty school district in the Midwest. As an Executive Director for School Support and Supervision, Scott directly supports a wide variety of elementary schools and settings, providing guidance to principals and their leadership teams on all aspects of running schools. In addition, Scott supports leadership development programs, principal mentoring, and new principal support in his district. Scott's doctoral work was centered on principal mentoring for instructional leadership. He has also worked as a mentor teacher, technology coach, and facilitated school-wide behavior management programs in schools where he taught and led. In his free moments, he enjoys time with his two elementary age boys, his beautiful wife and her dog, and all the soccer games and practices that can be fit into his life.